MW00533570

"Do you have challeng[...]
Here is an easy shortcut[...]

1. Order David C[...]
   Anxious Brain.

2. Start reading it, a few pages at a time. Carbonell writes with humor and compassion. I challenge you to read his book without smiling!

3. Highlight, circle, or use Post-its to mark the paragraphs that are especially helpful to you.

4. Make a habit of rereading the sections that you marked. You now have an ongoing resource for your progress!"

—**Neal Sideman**, self-help advocate, member of the Anxiety and Depression Association of America (ADAA), and cochair of the ADAA Public Education Committee

"Another gem of a book from David Carbonell. He writes with such wisdom and clarity, using delightful and memorable metaphors to help you outsmart your anxiety. He presents ten simple yet profound ways to get your life back. I highly recommend this book!"

—**Jennifer Shannon, LMFT**, author of *Don't Feed the Monkey Mind*

"Whether you have social anxiety, obsessive-compulsive disorder (OCD), panic attacks, or another form of anxiety, David Carbonell effortlessly explains the common culprit in all anxiety disorders in this essential read. Sprinkled with good humor, practical analogies, and real-life examples, he offers strategic tips that challenge your worries and change your anxious mind-set. A must-read based on empirical evidence for anyone looking to outsmart the anxiety tornado from wrecking your mental wellness."

> —**Jenny C. Yip, PsyD, ABPP**, founder and clinical
> psychologist at the Renewed Freedom Center for
> Rapid Anxiety Relief in Los Angeles, CA; and
> author of *Productive, Successful YOU!*

"David Carbonell has spent decades figuring out exactly how to explain complex and subtle concepts in just a few words, and this book is a prime example. Deceptively easygoing, it turns upside down every instinctive response to anxiety in the mind or body, and convinces the reader to behave counterintuitively. He articulates basic principles we so often overlook, such as that the rules for achieving goals in external reality and internal experience are not the same. Or that 'face your fears' does not mean confrontation, it means working *with* instead of against. This is a must-read!"

> —**Sally Winston, PsyD**, coauthor (with Martin Seif)
> of *Overcoming Unwanted Intrusive Thoughts* and
> *Needing to Know for Sure*

"This book will change lives. No one else explains worry and pre-scribes a clear path to lessen it like David Carbonell. His short, simple, and humorous book will help you understand how worry tricks you, while his writings give you powerful, specific techniques to reclaim your life from the anxiety that has been holding you back."

> —**Marilee Feldman, LCPC, CADC**, founder and clinical director of Life Counseling Institute in Willowbrook, IL

"This wonderful book gives the reader practical tips to move past anxiety and worry. David Carbonell offers sage advice on how to do things you are afraid of so that you become less afraid, rather than waiting to be less afraid so that you can do the things that are most important to you."

> —**Debra Kissen, PhD, MHSA**, CEO of Light On Anxiety CBT Treatment Center

"David Carbonell's sequel to *The Worry Trick* applies his practical advice not only to chronic worriers, but also to sufferers of panic, OCD, social anxiety, and phobias. With his witty, clear, and casual voice—and his memorable metaphors and exercises—he helps readers to stop treating discomfort like danger. I will enthusiasti-cally recommend this book to my anxious patients (and friends!)."

> —**David J. Kosins, PhD**, psychologist in private practice in Seattle, WA, clinical instructor in the University of Washington's departments of psychology and psychiatry; and founding fellow and certified trainer/consultant at the Academy of Cognitive Therapy

"As someone who has a history of anxiety and phobias, and as someone who is a social worker and has been director of an anxiety and phobia program for over twenty years, I will wholeheartedly recommend David Carbonell's new book to my colleagues and clients. Carbonell has an exceptional gift for presenting practical, therapeutic instruction and education with a sense of humor and a compassionate heart."

—**Judy Chessa, LMSW**, coordinator of the anxiety and phobia program at St. Vincent's Hospital Behavioral Health Services in White Plains, NY

"David Carbonell's new book, *Outsmart Your Anxious Brain*, is just what the doctor ordered. David has distilled much of the recent literature on how best to manage anxiety into an accessible and very readable book. David has done an excellent job of combining the wisdom he has gained from over thirty years' experience treating anxiety disorders with recent findings in the research literature to create a very practical book that is full of clinical insights and specific, concrete tools to better understand and manage anxiety. I especially like how David provides exercises to try, and then gives examples of how some of the clients in his practice have used and benefited from those exact exercises. If you or someone you care about suffers from anxiety—buy, read, and use this book! I'm eagerly awaiting the publication of this book so I can recommend it to my clients."

—**Robert W. McLellarn, PhD**, founder and director of Anxiety and Panic Treatment Center, LLC in Portland, OR; with over thirty years of experience treating anxiety disorders

"David is back with his signature style of warmth and humor to help readers work with anxiety moment by moment. From years of treating anxious people like you and me, he has come to see that avoidance behaviors are the problem, not anxiety. Want to know the secret to recovering faster? Look at what anxiety is telling you to do and do the opposite.

Take it chapter by chapter, grab a pencil to write in the margins, and then get out there and take back your life. It's been waiting for you!"

—**Kristin E. Cummings, LCSW**, resident superhero at www.theanxietygirl.net

Outsmart Your Anxious Brain

10 Simple Ways to Beat the Worry Trick

David A. Carbonell, PhD

New Harbinger Publications, Inc.

Publisher's Note

This publication is designed to provide accurate and authoritative information in regard to the subject matter covered. It is sold with the understanding that the publisher is not engaged in rendering psychological, financial, legal, or other professional services. If expert assistance or counseling is needed, the services of a competent professional should be sought.

In consideration of evolving American English usage standards, and reflecting a commitment to equity for all genders, "they/them" is used in this book to denote singular persons.

NEW HARBINGER PUBLICATIONS is a registered trademark of New Harbinger Publications, Inc.

Distributed in Canada by Raincoast Books

Copyright © 2020 by David A. Carbonell
New Harbinger Publications, Inc.
5674 Shattuck Avenue
Oakland, CA 94609
www.newharbinger.com

Cover design by Amy Shoup; Acquired by Tesilya Hanauer;
Edited by Gretel Hakanson

All Rights Reserved

Library of Congress Cataloging-in-Publication Data

Printed in the United States of America

25   24   23

10   9   8   7   6   5   4

For Ellen

Contents

Foreword

Got worries? Read this book. Do you have loved ones with worries? Have them read this book. Are you a professional who treats worried clients? Then you should definitely read this book, and give copies to your clients. They will thank you for it.

Did you know that worry plays tricks, and that's why it's so hard to get rid of it? In this wonderful new book, Dr. Dave Carbonell explains the worry trick to you in simple, clear, concise language that will stick in your head and come to your mind when you need it. And then he explains how to beat that trick: the principles that will guide your recovery and the specific actions that will make it come about.

Anxiety treatment has undergone a dramatic transformation since sufferers were told to change their thoughts, learn relaxation, practice thought stopping, or reduce their stress. These aren't bad ideas—but they just don't stop worry—and you probably have already discovered that. In *Outsmart Your Anxious Brain: Ten Simple Ways to Beat the Worry Trick*, Dave will teach you ways that are both proven and effective.

Dave has been at the forefront of the most innovative and effective forms of anxiety treatment, and his position as a leader is solidified with this newest book. His observations are astute. One intriguing example: he asks you not to call it a panic attack. That's because it doesn't attack you. Would you fall in love and say that you are having a "love attack"? Dave suggests you see panic as an experience because calling it an attack makes you want to fight back. But fighting against anxiety makes it stronger. That's one of its tricks. Dave will explain it to you and show you how to beat that trick.

Dave takes the most complicated, nuanced aspects of anxiety treatment and manages to present them in a way that is startlingly clear (you will find yourself saying often while reading this book, "Oh, of course! That's exactly true. Why didn't I see that before?"). And then he mixes that with his unique brand of humor. He'll explain the "rope-a-dope" method for coping with worry (and how to avoid being the dope!), why it's better to humor than argue with your worries, the benefits of turning your worries into haikus or limericks, and the essential differences between distraction (not so good) and observation (much better!) in learning to beat the worry trick. The result is a book that takes an immense amount of information about modern anxiety treatment and distills it into ten simple ways to beat the trick.

Along the way, Dave presents the Rule of Opposites, the essential components of therapeutic exposure (which he calls "practice"), a list of the ways that anxiety tricks you, a reminder to focus on what you do and not what you feel, and a suggestion that it is usually better to breathe out when anxious than to breathe in. That's right: don't always believe those that tell you to take a "deep breath."

In the words of Dr. Carbonell, anxiety is counterintuitive. He introduces a concrete and effective method of using his insights while practicing his suggestions for beating the worry trick. Dave points them out with the acronym AWARE, a five-step process to conduct during a practice session or during any experience of high anxiety. The steps involve accept, watch, act, repeat, and end. I especially like the "end" aspect since it emphasizes the reality that all anxiety experiences have a beginning, a middle, and an end—a truism that runs counter to the oft-felt experience of anxiety as an "endless nightmare."

In an important and unique chapter, Dr. Carbonell discusses the role of shame and secrecy in maintaining worries. Shame and secrecy, he points out, work together to energize anxious worries by aiding and abetting avoidance and distraction. Dave goes over the pros and cons of keeping worries private (secrecy) versus being reasonably honest and open about one's anxieties (self-disclosure) and gives concrete suggestions for sensible experiments with self-disclosure.

Outsmart Your Anxious Brain: Ten Simple Ways to Beat the Worry Trick is Dr. Carbonell at his best: succinct, humorous, perceptive, creative, and supportive. I am flattered and honored to introduce this book to you, with the assurance that you will finish reading it with a new perspective and a grasp of tools for overcoming toxic worries and the torments they produce.

> —Martin N. Seif, PhD, cofounder of Anxiety and Depression Association of America and coauthor of *What Every Therapist Needs to Know About Anxiety Disorders, Overcoming Unwanted Intrusive Thoughts,* and *Needing to Know for Sure.*

Introduction

We live in an "age of anxiety" in which about 45 million Americans—and hundreds of millions of people around the globe—suffer with a chronic anxiety disorder. An anxiety disorder isn't simply a condition of having lots of anxiety. It's a condition in which your struggle with anxiety and worry becomes a major element of daily life.

A person with an anxiety disorder comes to treat anxiety not just as symptoms of nervousness but as a threat. The experience of anxiety and the efforts to not have that experience combine to form a vicious cycle of anticipating anxiety symptoms, fearing them, resisting and avoiding them, experiencing them anyway, dreading them all the more, and actually bringing more anxiety into your life with your efforts to stop worrying.

You can recover from a chronic anxiety disorder by finding ways to interrupt and break that vicious cycle. Here in this book are ten simple ways you can do that.

There are several distinct anxiety disorders: panic disorder, social anxiety disorder, generalized anxiety disorder, obsessive-compulsive disorder, and all manner of phobias. One thing they have in common is that when people review their difficult situation and their efforts to break free of anxiety, they are likely to observe, with despair, that "the harder I try, the worse it gets!"

Our natural tendency to resist and avoid anxiety takes ordinary anxiety and pumps it up into an anxiety disorder. We get into a counterproductive struggle with our anxiety symptoms: worrisome thoughts, uncomfortable physical sensations, reflexive behaviors, and negative emotions. We treat anxiety, panic, and worry like an external threat, rather than an internal reaction. We resist it when it appears, and we worry about it appearing when it's not present. We develop an argumentative, confrontational relationship with anxiety, which unfortunately makes it worse rather than better. The path to overcoming chronic anxiety disorders is to develop a more adaptive way of relating to anxiety, and that's what this book will help you do.

Even the way we describe and label anxiety is often unhelpful and counterproductive. What we call a "panic attack" isn't an attack at all. It's a *reaction*. Sometimes the person experiencing panic doesn't even know what they're reacting to, but that still doesn't make it an attack of any kind. When we think we're being attacked, we naturally leap to defend ourselves. That effort to defend, when there's nothing in the present situation to defend against, is what keeps stirring the pot and making life worse.

The term "anxiety disorders" itself is misleading. Anxiety isn't the hallmark of anxiety disorders. Resistance and struggle against anxiety are the hallmarks of anxiety disorders. The next time the DSM (the guidebook to psychological disorders) gets revised, the term should be replaced. What we presently call "anxiety disorders" could be more appropriately labeled "disorders of excessive self-protection" because that's how they actually work.

Counterintuitive Problems

Chronic anxiety is a counterintuitive problem. If your puppy gets off the leash and runs down the street, your gut instinct is probably to run after him. But that only makes him run faster, as he enjoys the game of being chased. If you turn around and run away from the puppy, he'll chase you, and the situation gets resolved.

When people respond to this counterintuitive problem of anxiety in *intuitive ways*—just like running after the puppy—it usually makes their anxiety worse rather than better. The intuitive choice is usually to oppose what you don't want. But opposing your unwanted thoughts, emotions, and sensations will usually lead you to feel worse rather than better.

If you decide you don't like the clothes you're wearing, you can take them off and put on something else. The clothes you removed won't slither back onto your body. But if you decide you don't like the thoughts or physical sensations you're experiencing and try to get rid of them, maybe with thought stopping or even positive affirmations, those unwanted symptoms are likely to come right back and reenter your mind and body.

You can throw away objects you don't want, put them in the trash, and they won't come back. Not so with unwanted thoughts, emotions, and physical sensations—the more you try to rid yourself of them, the more persistently they will return. That's just how we're built. If it's true for you that "the harder I try, the worse it gets," it probably doesn't mean there's anything wrong with you. It probably means there's something wrong with the *methods* you're using to relieve your anxiety.

Anxiety symptoms tend to be uncomfortable at best and can seem so overbearing that they fool you into treating the anxiety as a threat. People who experience a strong level of anxiety don't like it and naturally want it to go away, the same way a driver skidding on an icy road and heading toward a utility pole will desperately want to stop the skid. A driver who stomps on the brake pedal in an effort to stop the skid will probably ensure a collision because the intended solution—stepping on the brake—actually magnifies the skid rather than stopping it. In the same way, people's characteristic efforts to stop anxiety tend to produce the opposite result, strengthening anxiety symptoms rather than relieving them.

The hallmark of a chronic anxiety disorder is that people are continually feeling afraid when they're not in any particular danger at that moment. This is why people come to my office, and the offices of thousands of professionals across the country, and it's probably why you are reading this book now. People recognize that their anxiety and worry do not provide a useful, timely signal of danger that they can use to protect themselves. Instead, they interject a chronic, repetitive *false alarm* into their lives. When they take that alarm at face value and try to protect themselves, it makes their lives less manageable and less enjoyable without enhancing their safety in any way. They give up a great deal of their freedom and activities and get no increased safety in return. It's a terribly bad trade. This is why people want so desperately to overcome a chronic anxiety disorder.

The Worry Trick

An anxiety disorder develops, and comes to full bloom, when a person falls into the pattern of treating the discomfort of anxiety as if it were danger. That's the fundamental "trick" of a chronic anxiety disorder: treating discomfort like danger. The reason people with anxiety disorders have so much trouble overcoming these problems is because they literally get tricked into responding to anxiety in ways they hope will calm it, but that actually make it more difficult and more persistent. In my first book, *Panic Attacks Workbook*[1], I explained how people could defuse the trick of panic attacks to overcome the fears and phobias of panic disorder. In my second, *The Worry Trick*[2], I explained how people could defuse the trick of chronic worry to overcome the obsessive worry often associated with generalized anxiety disorder.

People with panic disorder get tricked into treating their physical symptoms—changes in heart rate, labored breathing, chest tightness, and so on—as a sign of imminent danger. People with generalized anxiety disorder get tricked into treating their worrisome what-if thoughts as a sign of future danger. In each case, they struggle and oppose these symptoms, hoping to feel better, only to discover they feel worse. They will do better with a counterintuitive response, working *with* the anxiety and worry rather than against them.

Anxiety comes in a variety of symptoms—physical sensations, worried thoughts, fearful emotions, and reflexive behaviors—which all share the same meaning: "I'm nervous and afraid." They're different expressions of the same condition of being nervous. The experience of sweaty palms, for instance, means the same thing as fearful thoughts of fainting or labored breathing. They're different ways of experiencing nervousness, just like there are different flavors of ice cream. When we get tricked by anxiety and worry, we stop treating it like nervousness and start treating it like danger. That's what makes things worse rather than better.

In this book, I will show you how people with all manner of troubles with worry, fear, panic, and anxiety can outsmart the tricks that anxiety and worry persistently throw at them with ten practical responses. A fish that learns to notice the hook attached to that tempting food dangling in the water will learn not to take the bait, and that's what you can learn here. When you learn to notice the trick inherent in your anxiety and develop the habit of responding with a counter-intuitive response, that's when you can return your time, attention, and energy to all the interests and activities that used to be important to you before the trick of chronic anxiety entered your life. I'll show you ten simple ways you can defuse, rather than oppose, the anxiety that troubles you so.

How People Get Tricked

People think of anxiety as an enemy, and that's how they treat it. We only have three kinds of responses for dangerous enemies: fight, flight, and freeze. If it looks weaker than me, I'll fight it. If it looks stronger than me but slower, I'll run away from it. And if it looks stronger than me and faster than me, I'll freeze and hope it doesn't see well. That's all we have for enemies: fight, flight, and freeze. These are good responses…when you're actually in danger.

When you're not in danger, though, these instinctive responses of fight, flight, and freeze will lead you to feel more anxious over time, rather than less. Running away from or fighting off the attack of a predatory animal is a good thing because it can make you safer. Running away from a grocery store when you feel panicky there or trying to repel scary thoughts, for example, are unhelpful responses. They won't make you any safer, just more anxious.

Is it danger or discomfort? This is the question I would ask you if we were together when you started feeling high anxiety, and it's an excellent question to ask yourself when you're starting to experience a panic attack or other episode of high anxiety. "Discomfort" might seem like too mild a word for what you're experiencing, I know. (But I had to call it something, and I wanted another word that began with a *D* to make it easy to remember!) This question, "Is it danger or discomfort?" might be the best opportunity you get to immediately set out on a helpful path in response to a moment of high anxiety. If you treat the anxiety like a danger, fighting or fleeing it, that actually produces more anxiety rather than less. Treat the anxiety like discomfort though, and you'll be on the right track.

Consider, for instance, a person who feels short of breath and gets nervous about that. She might try hard to stop thinking of the word "breathing" only to find herself thinking it even more. She might strain to gulp more air, only to

Outsmart Your Anxious Brain

find her chest getting tighter and her breath getting shorter. She'll feel more anxious as a result of her effort, rather than less, because she's doing the anxiety equivalent of chasing the runaway puppy. Eventually the anxiety will diminish anyway. But imagine how much more useful it would be to recognize both the labored breathing and the worrisome thoughts about it as signs of discomfort, rather than danger, as something you can accept and work with rather than oppose. That's what I hope my question can remind you to do.

Outsmarting the Worry Trick

How can you outsmart the worry trick? You can do this by taking the counterintuitive choice. The intuitive choice, treating it like danger, means opposing, resisting, and fleeing the anxiety. The counterintuitive choice means treating it like discomfort. The best way to counter discomfort is with some version of "chill out and give it time to pass." Claire Weekes, an Australian physician who was the first person to write, helpfully, to a worldwide audience of anxiety sufferers back in the 1960s, used the metaphor "float" (with or through your anxiety), as opposed to "swim" (against the current of your anxiety). Weekes's advice, which still compares favorably with the most effective anxiety treatments today, suggests that you make no effort against worry and anxiety; you simply allow the environment to support you, just as one does in floating upon a body of water.[3]

What gives the anxiety trick so much power is that the responses that are useful for danger—fight, flight, and freeze—are pretty much the *opposite* of the responses that are useful for discomfort. So when you treat a discomfort as if it were a danger, you're responding in ways that make it feel worse rather than better. This is why people hold their breath during a panic attack. That won't actually help! This is why they try so hard to change or remove the thoughts they don't want, snapping rubber bands on their wrists and trying to distract themselves with another topic, only to get further embroiled with the unwanted thought. This is why they try so hard to "escape" from situations that aren't dangerous, like long lines at a grocery store or crowded churches or movie theaters. They're trying to protect themselves from a danger that doesn't exist at that time and place, and that's why they're feeling more afraid! It's almost as if they've literally been sabotaged into acting in ways that will give them the very thoughts and feelings they don't want.

Instead, if you can come to recognize the fear and anxiety as signs of discomfort, rather than danger, and respond accordingly, that will be the basis of a more helpful way of relating to worry and anxiety. That will truly be the path out.

One of the most striking characteristics of an anxiety disorder is that the terrible outcomes people fear tend not to happen. Has this been your experience?

Outsmart Your Anxious Brain

The Fears of Anxiety Disorders

Panic disorder:

- What if I have a heart attack?

- What if I go crazy?

- What if I pass out?

- What if I lose control of myself?

Obsessive-compulsive disorder:

- What if my neighborhood burns because I forgot to turn off the stove?

- What if people die of poisoning because I mis-handled the insecticide?

- What if I run over a pedestrian without noticing while I'm driving?

- What if I get poked by an HIV-infected needle sticking out of a trash can?

- What if I get germs or contaminants on my hands and my family gets sick?

- What if I hurt my children?

Social anxiety disorder:

- What if I freak out and have a meltdown in front of my coworkers?

- What if I look so nervous at the grocery store that people think I'm crazy?

- What if I get panicky in the restaurant but can't find an excuse for leaving?

- What if I break into a sweat while giving a presentation?

- What if I can't urinate in the office bathroom?

Generalized anxiety disorder:

- What if I get cancer?

- What if I lose my job? My spouse? My home?

- What if my thoughts drive me crazy?

You name it! If people can think of it, they'll imagine something terrible happening.

Specific phobias:

- What if a dog attacks me?

- What if I freak out on the airplane?

- What if I lose the ability to sleep?

- What if I have to stay at a hotel penthouse and am forced to use the elevator?

- What if I drive off a bridge?

And then, if you're like the other millions of people who suffer with an anxiety disorder, the episode passes, with you none the worse for wear, in the sense that, once again, you didn't die or go crazy. You didn't burn down the neighborhood, didn't make a humiliating display of yourself at the PTA meeting...but unfortunately, you're probably even more afraid of future disaster than you were before. Each and every time, when you have a peak anxiety episode, it fails to deliver the feared consequence. That's what makes this an anxiety disorder, rather than a death disorder, an insanity disorder, a fire-starting disorder, and so on.

So here's the central question of an anxiety disorder: Why don't people see this pattern—of fearing something that never seems to happen—and gradually lose their fear of it? Why don't they notice they're getting tricked and just naturally move past it?

I don't ask this question because I think people "should" be able to do this. I know they don't, and probably can't, without additional work. Sometimes friends and family ask anxiety patients this question, and people with an anxiety disorder may well feel defensive in response. But this is an important question because the answer reveals a great deal about how an anxiety disorder works and points to a more productive way of relating to anxiety. It will be a big help to discover the answer to this question, and we'll do that in the next chapter.

How to Use This Book

This book will help you find the tricky aspects of chronic anxiety disorders so you can start handling them in ways that shrink them down rather than build them up. Here you will find ways—ten simple ways—to shrink anxiety down to more manageable proportions.

I've been working as a professional psychologist for thirty years helping people overcome all kinds of fears and phobias. I didn't learn this in graduate school. I learned it from my clients—people who suffered with panic attacks, phobias of all kinds, chronic worry, intrusive thoughts and compulsive efforts to get rid of those thoughts, and social anxiety. Here, in this book, are some of the most important lessons they taught me.

The first two chapters provide background that will help you use the ten steps in the chapters that follow. Some readers will prefer to jump right into the techniques rather than read the background. If you're willing to read the chapters in order, I think that's the best. But if you're more of an action-oriented person who wants to start as soon as possible, that's also okay. You can come back to the first two chapters later if you feel the need.

The rest of the book—chapters 3 through 12—will introduce you to ten powerful techniques you can use to undo the worry trick and handle all forms of anxiety—thoughts, physical sensations, emotions, and behaviors—in ways that allow it to diminish and fade. The unfortunate experience of most anxiety sufferers is that they find their efforts to oppose and relieve the anxiety often escalate the problem, rather than relieve it. This book will show you how to turn that around.

I suggest you get yourself a notebook to take some notes and write answers to questions contained within this book.

Ready to move on? Let's find out why anxiety disorders don't typically just go away on their own.

PART   I

The Basics

Chapter 1

What Maintains Chronic Worry?

Why don't people notice how they're getting tricked by anxiety, panic, and worry and just naturally move past it?

This question bedevils the sufferers of chronic anxiety disorders. They fear the answer is that they're defective in some way—too weak, too cowardly, too stupid, and so on.

The truth is none of those. They don't get over it because they get blinded by their reliance on safety behaviors and other factors, which prevents them from seeing the problem and its solution clearly.

Susan first experienced a panic attack nearly three years ago. Since then, she's had more than twenty full-blown panic attacks. Each time she has one, she fears that she will faint, fall to the ground, be unable to breathe, and die. She has come to avoid many of the situations where she fears having an attack: crowded stores and events, standing in line, any significant amount of walking, hairstyling appointments, and more. Those she doesn't avoid, she endures with difficulty and the company of a trusted friend. Every attack has ended without a faint, a fall, or any of the life-threatening results she fears. However, she continues to fear and avoid the possibility of another attack.

Kyle worries, frequently and fearfully, about his health. During the last two years, he has been terribly preoccupied with worries about dying young. He worries about having a heart attack even though, at twenty-seven, he has no significant risk factors for heart disease nor is there any history of heart disease in his family. He repeatedly visits numerous doctors and hospitals for various tests and examinations. The results of all his doctor visits, physical examinations, and tests indicate no problems, and his doctors repeatedly tell him that he is in good health. Still, he continues to worry about his heart and health.

Safety Behaviors

Why don't people notice this pattern—of frequently fearing a catastrophic result that never materializes—see it as an exaggerated fear, and gradually get over it? The answer is that they get fooled by their reliance on a variety of "safety behaviors" that blind them to what is actually occurring.

Safety behaviors are naturally occurring preparations and responses to moments of high anxiety: efforts at protecting ourselves from perceived danger. During the three years in which she experienced panic attacks, Susan never

Outsmart Your Anxious Brain

experienced the fainting, falling, and dying that she feared. However, because she avoided so many situations where she feared panic or visited them only with a trusted friend, she came to believe that her avoidance and trusted friend were all that stood between her and death. This belief—that she required avoidance and company to survive—prevented her from discovering that she wasn't as vulnerable as she believed. In Kyle's case, it was his repeated reliance on physical examinations and verbal reassurance from doctors that prevented him from discovering that he was healthy.

Two common types of safety behaviors are "support people" and "support objects." A person who is accompanied by a support person is usually willing to do more of life's activities than when they are alone. It's good that they can get to their activities, but unfortunately, the anxious person who relies on a support person comes to believe even more strongly that they can't cope on their own, and that's a bad thing.

Support People

Eleanor, a woman in her forties, came to one of my panic support groups and told us she had a terrible fear she would faint if she drove at night. The group met in the evening, so her attendance was surprising. We soon learned that she had a part-time job working an overnight shift at a nearby factory.

She had worked there three nights a week for ten years. I asked her if she had ever fainted while driving to work, and she said, "Not yet!" I pointed out that she had driven to this night job about fifteen hundred times in the past ten years and had never fainted, nor had she fainted while driving to our meeting. She was batting zero! I asked her how she explained her failure to faint, and she had a ready reply. She hadn't fainted because her husband would follow her to work in his car! As long as she could see him in the rearview mirror, she felt confident that she wouldn't faint...that time. But it didn't help her overcome the fear because she attributed her remaining conscious, and therefore her well-being, to his presence and not to her own ability to cope. The more she relied on him following her, the less she was able to recognize that she, not he, was taking care of business.

Support Objects

Bob was intensely claustrophobic, afraid of being confined in small spaces. There were very few vehicles he could tolerate as a passenger—no cabs, airplanes, buses, trains, elevators, and so on. He couldn't tolerate being in a long line or a crowd, nor would he go to a crowded theater or church service. He bought all his shirts a size larger than he needed because he hated the sensation of a shirt clinging tightly to him. However, there was nothing he enjoyed more in life than deep-sea diving. He enjoyed this activity above all others, descending fifty feet below the surface of a body of water into a dark, cold, murky climate in which his life depended on a tube of air connected to a boat above, monitored by a friend who, for all he knew, might be enjoying a cold beer.

You might wonder how a claustrophobic person could tolerate, let alone enjoy, deep-sea diving. Here is how he did it. The first preparation he would make for a dive was to attach to his ankle, in a waterproof bag, a Xanax. Then he would put on his full-body wetsuit, flippers, breathing apparatus, and all the other equipment. The Xanax, in his view, is what enabled him to enter into this environment.

You can probably see that the prospect of him being able to swallow the Xanax underwater was pretty poor. That didn't matter! In fact, that was even better because he was afraid of becoming addicted to Xanax if he took them often. Medications are frequently used as support objects. Some people carry the same bottle of Xanax with them for years without ever ingesting a single pill. They don't have to! Just carrying those expired medications gives them the relief they seek.

Safety behaviors trick you. When you rely on them, you get fooled into believing that something—a person, an object, avoidance, distraction, and a few others—protected you from harm and that, if that safety behavior or object weren't available, then you would suffer a calamity. The more you rely on safety behaviors, the more vulnerable and dependent you feel because you attribute your safety and well-being to the safety behaviors, as if they were bodyguards, rather than to your own ability to cope with life challenges. Reliance on safety behaviors deprives you of the opportunity to learn from your own experience.

Distraction and Thought Stopping

The use of support objects and support people isn't the only safety behavior people employ. There's also distraction and thought stopping. People often discover the "value" of distraction when something happens around them while they're feeling anxious. Maybe your smoke alarm made sounds indicating the battery was low or your child fell down and got a bloody nose. These events naturally command your immediate attention, and it often happens that the anxiety immediately ends as a result. Later that day, when the smoke alarm or child are back to normal, you might remember that you were starting to feel panicky and realize that the distraction chased it away. From that moment on, distraction might seem like your friend, and you might make deliberate efforts to "stop thinking about anxiety."

One problem with this, of course, is that while distraction works well when it's a spontaneous response, it works poorly when we try to deliberately and consciously distract ourselves from something. Our effort to distract, our self-instruction to "stop thinking about it," serves to remind us of the exact idea we don't want to think about. This is why the most likely result of trying to suppress your thoughts is to have more of the thoughts you are trying to suppress.

An even bigger problem with relying on distraction is that it contains within it the idea that thoughts can be dangerous. Thoughts aren't dangerous. Only actions can be dangerous. For example, driving off a bridge is dangerous. Having what-if thoughts about driving off a bridge, on the other hand, may be uncomfortable, unpleasant, and scary, but not dangerous. Your auto insurance premium won't go up simply because you experience those what-if thoughts! What's more, when you focus on distracting yourself in an anxious condition, it interferes with your ability to observe what actually happens and learn from that experience.

Rituals and Superstitions

Relying on rituals and superstitions is another safety behavior. It's common, for instance, for people who fear flying to engage in minor rituals, like touching the skin of the airplane before they board, always reserving the same row number to sit in, flying on a particular day of the week, or wearing their lucky shirt. "Why not?" they reason. "It can't hurt!" But rituals and superstitions do hurt. They perpetuate the idea that you have to do something to make yourself safer when you're probably already as safe as you can be. They create more items on a checklist that they think they need to monitor to be okay, rather than simply showing up, taking their seat, and allowing the crew to do their job of safely taking them to their destination.

Avoidance

This safety behavior is perhaps the most important one of all. It's so obvious that you might overlook it, the way we often fail to notice something staring us in the face. It's avoidance and escape, the pattern of staying away from, and fleeing, the object, activity, situation, or location you fear. The more you avoid the things that trigger your fear, the more persistent and strong the anxiety becomes over time. Maybe you avoid the highway entrance ramp, if you're afraid of highways; bridges and tunnels, if you fear those; parties and meetings, if you fear social encounters and observation; the kitchen, if you fear your own obsessive thoughts about knives or stoves; a doctor visit for an annual physical, if you fear thinking or hearing about your own physical health; or even hearing or reading about a particular topic, like mental health, if you fear your own thoughts about insanity.

It's true that you'll feel better as you turn away from those cues. The problem is that the comfort you get usually doesn't last more than a few moments. Your fears about the next time you encounter a highway, bridge, party, kitchen knife, or whatever, will unfortunately keep growing and recurring. When you avoid, you get a few moments of temporary, brief comfort at the price of giving up your long-term freedom, and it's a terribly bad trade. That's probably why you want to overcome the anxiety disorder, because you've given up so much of your life in your effort to control the anxiety, and you have so little to show for what you've sacrificed.

Safety Behaviors Don't Work

When people with anxiety disorders come to see me for the first time, they often tell me this: "Despite my best efforts, my anxiety keeps getting worse." They mean this sincerely, but it's not really true. Here's what's true: their anxiety keeps getting worse *because of* their best efforts. Their best efforts usually include a variety of safety behaviors: actions they hope will protect them but which actually only lead them to feel more vulnerable over time. Safety behaviors are wolves in sheepdogs' clothing. They look like they're coming to the rescue, but they're not on your side! Reducing your reliance on safety behaviors is one of the most helpful steps you can take.

This is where the idea of "face your fears" comes from. Safety behaviors and objects offer to "protect" you from your fears but actually strengthen them. Practice, or *exposure* to what you fear, will gradually remove the fears. But the spirit in which you do the exposure is just as important as the exposure itself. I don't like the phrase "face your fears." It sounds too much like a confrontation—a staring contest, a toe-to-toe argument, or a physical struggle with an external opponent. That's not the spirit that's best suited for overcoming these fears. Working *with*, rather than *against*, your signs and symptoms of anxiety is a much more helpful attitude to take when you do exposure work.

How Your Thoughts Trick You

There are several ways that your thoughts, and particularly the habitual ways you relate to your thoughts, can serve to build and maintain the worry trick. These worry habits can sabotage your efforts to live the life you want. Changing the ways you relate to your worrisome thoughts will help you get fooled less frequently.

Anticipating the Worst

First and foremost is the experience of anticipatory worry. Most people with chronic anxiety disorders experience far more than their share of anticipatory worry, and much of it is subliminal. It's worry that occurs in the back of the mind, and the middle as well, and people often don't even notice that it's occurring. The worry drones on and on, as people multitask and engage in various other activities, and they start feeling nervous and uncomfortable without knowing why. It will be a big help to become a better observer of your own anticipatory worry, to literally catch it in the act, so you can practice different responses to the worry habit.

Did you just have a thought that you don't want to notice the worry? That the last thing you want to do is notice it? You might suppose you'd feel better if you didn't notice it, but it's probably the other way around. When you notice that you're engaging in the worry habit, there are helpful things you can do, but when you don't particularly notice, the worry can go on and on.

Here's something that will help you catch yourself in the act of automatic worry: the great majority of worrisome anticipatory thoughts start with the words "what if." This will literally be the signal, like a starter pistol at a race, that the worry habit has intruded once again. You might suppose that you're better off if you didn't notice, but I think you'll find you have more and better options to tame this habit when you notice it.

Misattribution

Misattribution is another important element in our thinking style that maintains a chronic anxiety disorder. Have you ever had the experience of starting to feel a panic attack coming on while waiting in a long line at a grocery or hardware store? Sometimes it happens that, just as you think all is lost, the manager comes on the PA system and invites shoppers to move to a new cashier line that just opened up. Or sometimes the spell of panic is broken as you receive an unexpected phone call from a support person.

Those events—the unexpected call or the opening of a new line—seem at the time to be a blessing because they appear to have rescued you from the grim prospect of a panic attack. Many people who experience them will believe that they "got through" the attack because of these unexpected events. Or, more generally, people will feel they were "lucky" to get through an attack without calamity and attribute their survival and subsequent well-being to luck.

The problem is that when you attribute your survival to a chance element in the environment, be it luck or the availability of another underpaid cashier, this probably leads you to feel more anxious and insecure about the future, rather than less. It makes it seem like you just survived an incident that could have done something terrible to you, and you made it through only because of the presence of this element.

People who fall into this pattern don't feel better about their future prospects; they feel worse. Each and every time they survive and attribute it to the beneficial impact of some element in the environment, they feel more vulnerable going forward rather than less because what if that element isn't available next time? You can see this very clearly when people attribute their survival in an encounter with anxiety to "luck." How do people feel about their future when they believe they've survived so far by being "lucky"? They feel worse because they figure that sooner or later, they will literally "run out of luck"!

Misunderstandings About Control

Confusion about "control issues" and unhelpful efforts to "be in control" also serve to maintain and aggravate a chronic anxiety disorder. People who struggle with chronic anxiety disorders often suppose that when they're experiencing powerful negative emotions and persistent disturbing thoughts, it means they're out of control. A person with panic disorder who experiences a panic attack while driving may be very upset by the idea that she's "out of control" while driving. She may fear that she will lose control of herself and the vehicle and cause a terrible accident. This person may start to avoid driving, particularly on divided highways and other roads that don't allow her to get off the road anytime she wants.

Control isn't measured by what you think and feel. Control is measured by what you do. When I talk with a client who fears being "out of control" while experiencing a panic attack on a highway, I want to know how the client actually handles the car. I usually ask: "If I were a policeman following you, would I see your vehicle doing anything that would lead me to pull you over? For instance, were you driving at speeds that varied considerably from that of the other cars nearby? Were you changing lanes without signaling or failing to stay within your lane? Were you maneuvering without use of your mirrors and cutting people off? Did you fail to have your headlights on at night or drive in traffic with your brights on? Did you hear multiple drivers honking at your violation of driving laws and norms?"

Those kinds of driving behaviors are signs of a driver not appropriately in control. Having strong, even upsetting emotions, on the other hand, is not a sign of being out of control, nor is having unwanted intrusive thoughts, however scary and upsetting. Control is measured by behavior. When you're driving, that's indicated by what you are actually doing and what your car is doing.

What does it mean to have a panic attack while driving even as you handle the vehicle appropriately, displaying no behaviors that would attract the attention of a policeman? It means that you're driving while nervous. It's okay to drive while nervous—not enjoyable, not something to aspire to, but nothing that warrants reliance on safety behaviors that will make your life more difficult over time. It's okay to feel nervous. As you get better at allowing, and accepting, those thoughts and signs of nervousness, they will probably diminish over time.

Two More Saboteurs: Shame and Secrecy

Keeping your fears and anxieties a secret is another way you might try to help yourself, which instead aggravates the problem. People who struggle with chronic anxiety disorders often feel ashamed and embarrassed about their fears. They usually try to hide them and keep them a secret. Secrecy is the flip side of shame. The more shame a person feels, the more they struggle to hide their troubles. And, as you probably know, the more you try to hide your problems, the more shame you're likely to feel about them.

This reliance on secrecy is why we have millions of people with chronic anxiety disorders, all thinking that they're the only one, or at least one of the very worst cases. Secrecy prevents people from discovering how common these problems are. Secrecy prevents people from discovering that other people aren't usually as critical of their flaws as they suppose. Relying on secrecy leads people to focus more on hiding their problems than solving them, and this helps perpetuate the problem.

Thinking It Over

These are the reasons that anxiety disorders seem so hard to solve. It's not that the problem can't be solved. It's that the problem itself literally tricks you into treating it like a danger, and when you treat it like a danger, you act in ways that make it more severe and more persistent over time. It literally tricks you in the manner of the old saying about "putting out fires with gasoline."

Instead, if you can begin to treat it like discomfort, rather than danger, that's much more truly the path out. This is how you can change your relationship with chronic anxiety, panic, and worry. If you've been treating them like danger— avoiding, opposing, resisting, distracting from, and trying to protect yourself—then you've been relating to anxiety in ways that do make it worse over time.

Changing your relationship with anxiety, treating it more like the discomfort it is, is how you can regain your freedom from a chronic anxiety disorder.

The next chapter will introduce a powerful rule you can use to guide your selection and creation of responses to anxiety. This rule, the Rule of Opposites, will help you identify the types of responses that are most likely to be helpful when you're struggling with anxiety and worry.

Chapter 2

The Rule of Opposites

There's a powerful and surprising rule of thumb that pertains to all of our instinctive responses to anxiety, panic, and worry.

It's this: your (and my) initial gut instinct of how to respond to a strong anxiety episode is almost always wrong. Not just wrong, but precisely and completely wrong, 180 degrees wrong, like a compass that points north but labels it south.

If you have a compass like that, that's a problem, but there's an easy workaround. As long as you know that what the compass calls south is actually north, you can still find your way home. And so it is with the signs and symptoms of chronic anxiety disorders. If you can see that your gut instinct of how to respond to panic, worry, and anxiety is usually dead wrong, then that sets the stage for you to do the opposite next time that anxiety comes into play.

How Anxiety Tricks Your Brain

Why are our instinctive responses to worry and anxiety so reliably unhelpful? It goes to the heart of the worry trick: people experience discomfort and treat it like danger. The responses that are useful for danger—fight, flight, and freeze—are pretty much the opposite of what's useful for discomfort, essentially, to chill out, float, and give it time to pass. So when you get tricked into treating the discomfort of anxiety and worry as if it were danger, you get tricked into acting in ways that make your long-term situation worse rather than better. You get a few moments of temporary relief as you retreat from or resist the anxiety. But you end up feeling more afraid and vulnerable in the long term. You're giving up your long-term freedom for a few moments of very temporary relief and comfort. It's a terribly bad trade. Making those trades is exactly what keeps people stuck in anxiety disorders.

When people experience a moment of high anxiety, they tend to either try to fend off a "danger" that probably doesn't exist at that time and place, or try to oppose and silence their fear. Neither helps them calm down. Instead, they become more afraid and also upset with themselves for once again feeling overcome by fear.

People often worry that this means there's something wrong with them or with their brain. But this is actually evidence of your brain trying to carry out its job—keeping you safe—rather than any sign of malfunction. Our brains are much more willing to make the error of seeing a lion where there isn't one than of not seeing a lion where there is one. The first mistake just brings on some discomfort; the second one might lead to danger and death. So our brains will naturally choose to err on the side of seeing dangers that aren't there. The principal task of your brain is to protect you, not to keep you comfortable.

So don't be too concerned about *why* your brain so often predicts dangers that aren't there. It's just taking a very conservative approach to the task of keeping you alive, and it errs on the side of caution. This means it may frequently spur you to automatically react in ways that are unnecessary and that make you feel uncomfortable and anxious. That's just the way we're built, and some people have a little more of this tendency than others, just like some people are more sensitive to light, sound, and all other kinds of stimuli.

Using the Rule of Opposites to Defuse the Worry Trick

The Rule of Opposites says this: My gut instinct of how to respond to panic and high anxiety is typically dead wrong and following that instinct makes my troubles worse rather than better. So I will respond with the *opposite* of my gut instinct.

An example from my own life: I've never been comfortable with heights. It's much better today than it used to be, mostly because I worked at exposure when I was younger, but I still feel anxious even now when I find myself in high, open situations. My principal exposure practice was walking across large bridges when I had the opportunity, and the first time I did this was on the Golden Gate Bridge.

It's a bridge for both vehicles and pedestrians. It has sidewalks on both sides and a ten-foot fence for the first quarter of the bridge. I saw kids on bicycles there and was horrified to see that some of them were actually riding their bikes, not cautiously walking them across! I saw people walking dogs, and some of the dogs weren't even on a leash! There were joggers running across the bridge! And there were also a few older folks, using canes and walkers to take a stroll! They were all out there, walking, running, and riding across the bridge as if it were nothing!

And then there was me—going far slower than all of them. At first, I felt so terrified, so filled with physical fear, that I didn't believe I could continue. I was moving so slowly. I wanted to turn around but had some weird thoughts (I had a lot of weird thoughts on that first walk) that I might slip and lose control if I did so, as if the surface of the bridge were too slick to maneuver safely! Then I realized that I was moving so slowly because I was trying to keep my feet in contact with the surface of the bridge at all times. I wanted to feel grounded

Outsmart Your Anxious Brain

so badly that I was literally dragging my heels in order to feel connected to what passed for the ground up there!

No sooner did I notice this than I remembered the Rule of Opposites. And I was sorry I remembered the Rule of Opposites because the idea was scary. But this was the kind of thing I had often encouraged my clients to do, so I did what the Rule of Opposites suggested to me.

I hopped. It was pretty small as hops go. It probably deserved a mention in the Guinness World Records for world's shortest hop. And I did it while backed up by a ten-foot fence, so my chances of falling off the bridge were pretty poor! But it's hard to overstate what a sense of relief I got from this hop. You can't hop while holding your muscles tightly, and so I relaxed a lot of muscles that I'd been holding tight as a drum. That felt good. It was a silly thing to do and made me laugh. That felt good too. Nobody came running over, the way I thought they would, to stare at the crazy man hopping. And I was still there, with the ten-foot fence, and life went on just like before, after my little hop. I still had lots of fear to work through, but this made a big difference in enabling me to keep going.

That's how the Rule of Opposites can help you identify and use a helpful response when you're caught up in the worry trick.

Does this seem too radical or risky to you? It's not as radical as it might seem because the Rule of Opposites is meant to be used in response to very small, automatic responses that you can catch yourself using when caught up in a moment of high anxiety. It's not intended for major life decisions—whether or not to go to college, to get married, or to have a baby. It's something you apply to micro-behaviors that you can catch yourself in the act of doing during a moment of intense fear.

Examples of How to Use the Rule of Opposites

Driving fears. If you're afraid of driving, or fear having a panic attack while you drive, you'll probably find lots of ways the Rule of Opposites can be helpful. Many fearful drivers keep their fingers locked in a death grip around the steering wheel. Maybe they have the idea that this is necessary to maintain control of the car. Maybe having sweaty palms, another common anxiety symptom, leads them to fear their hands slipping off the wheel. Whatever the case, any driving instructor will tell you that keeping a relaxed, light grip on the wheel is the best, and the Rule of Opposites will take you in the same direction here.

So a fearful driver who notices this particular symptom of gripping the wheel so tightly can use the Rule of Opposites to identify a useful response to this death grip. The beauty of this is that you can take it one small step at a time. You can initially relax the pinky of your weak hand, if you want to take the smallest step possible, while allowing all the other fingers to maintain their death grip, and see how that small step affects your situation. Once you're satisfied that this doesn't disrupt your control of the car, and probably feels slightly better, you can relax some other fingers, going as gradually as you wish. (I've worked with several clients who enjoyed "giving fear the finger" as they came to their middle finger!)

Flying fears. In a similar manner, a fearful flyer can probably detect getting tricked into responding in a variety of unhelpful ways—gripping the armrest, keeping their eyes closed, or maybe covering their face with a towel in an effort to avoid noticing that they're on a plane, maintaining a crash position, and so on. Gripping the armrest might be helpful if you're actually being thrown around by turbulence but will simply make you feel more tense and nervous when you're not. You don't need to hold yourself in; that's what the seatbelt is for! Closing or covering your eyes will deprive you of information about what's actually occurring around you and leave you at the mercy of your worst imagined fears. Maintaining a crash position for an hour or more is going to leave you feeling cramped, tense, and vulnerable.

What would be the opposite of these responses? Relaxing your hands and letting them rest at your sides or in your lap will let you gradually relax a bit in ways that gripping the armrest never will. Allowing yourself to look around and notice the interior of the airplane, with passengers and crew, would be the opposite of covering your eyes, and you'll probably feel better as you view the actual situation around you, rather than the one you imagine with your eyes closed. Sitting back and letting the seat support your body will feel more calming than maintaining a crash position.

It's the same with thinking that it's so shameful to feel afraid of flying that you need to hide it. It's certainly uncomfortable to feel afraid, but it's perfectly okay to fly on a commercial airline while feeling afraid, just as it's okay to fly while feeling sad, happy, angry, jealous, tired, or whatever. We don't want the pilot to feel afraid, but it's okay to have passengers who are afraid. What's the opposite of trying to hide it? Telling someone! When we take a flight with my fearful flyers workshop, we always tell the crew we're a group of fearful flyers.

Public speaking fears. Fearful speakers can similarly catch themselves in the act of getting tricked into certain unhelpful responses—standing rigidly behind a podium and gripping the edges tightly, staring at their notes and avoiding eye contact with the audience, rushing in an effort to keep talking every moment and avoiding any pauses. The speaker would be well served to notice each of these micro-behaviors of anxiety and do the opposite—standing in a relaxed posture at the podium with hands at their sides or gently resting on the podium, looking out at the audience and making occasional eye contact with various individuals while referring to his notes without reading them or staring at them, and periodically pausing for a breath while giving the audience time to digest what they said. All of these are good counters to the worry trick.

The Rule of Opposites in the Moment

When you're caught up in a moment of high anxiety, you're likely to be excessively focused on your symptoms and lots of worrying about what to do and what the future holds. Your attention gets diverted from the immediate circumstances to lots of hypothetical problems that could happen in the future. The anxiety disrupts your ability to be an observer of your present experience and reality. You'll be better able to use the Rule of Opposites by turning your powers of observation back to your immediate circumstances. Use the following questions for a start.

What are you doing with:

- your hands?

- your shoulders?

- the muscles of your chest?

- your breathing?

- your posture?

Are you tensing and clenching parts of your body? Do you feel tension in your chest and shoulders? Is your breathing short and shallow? Notice the places where you're perhaps adding tension to your physical sensations. Consider what the Rule of Opposites has to offer about that. Gently do the opposites that occur to you, and then move on.

What are you:

- looking at?

- listening to?

- focused on?

- thinking about?

Where is your attention and energy?

- Is it focused inside your head, with all its what-if thoughts?

- Is it focused on your body, hypervigilant to every physical sensation?

What is there to observe around you? Take a few moments to turn your attention to the objects, sounds, colors, temperatures, and other details of your immediate environment.

Thinking It Over

The Rule of Opposites can be your most useful guide as you seek to reclaim your freedom from a chronic anxiety disorder. My clients find, again and again, that it's those moments when they catch themselves in the act of some small, intuitive response to anxiety—like tensing their shoulders or gripping the steering wheel—and do the opposite that are the turning points in their recovery. The idea of the opposites will turn up again and again in the rest of this book, and it underlies all the useful replies you can use when you're being tricked by worry and anxiety.

In the next chapter, we'll take a look at a specific behavior that's often a major source of anxiety—the labored, short, and shallow breathing that people experience as part of panic attacks and other forms of anxiety—and see how the Rule of Opposites can guide you to a solution.

PART II

Ways to Counter the Tricks of Worry and Anxiety

Chapter 3

Breathe Through Panic

Feeling short of breath is a hallmark of panic attacks. People try so hard to take a deep breath during a panic attack, only to find that their breathing usually feels worse rather than better.

What's the opposite of taking a deep breath? Giving one away! Let's see how this works.

Owen Gets Tricked

Owen was waiting impatiently for a staff meeting to start when he began to experience uncomfortable physical sensations. His face felt warm, his heart seemed to race, his chest felt tight, and he felt short of breath. Owen was no stranger to these sensations. In fact, he'd had several full-blown panic attacks in the past year. He hoped he wasn't about to have another one. The more Owen felt these symptoms, the more uncomfortable he got, and he started to worry that maybe he'd faint or even stop breathing completely and die of asphyxiation.

Owen felt as though his brain were literally screaming at him, "Take a deep breath!" And so he tried. He opened his mouth, tilted his head back, elevated his shoulders and chest, and struggled to inhale. Still, Owen felt like his breaths were getting shorter and shorter.

We'll interrupt Owen's story here. It may seem evident to you that he's probably about to have another panic attack. He's getting more and more frightened by the physical sensations he's experiencing, especially the labored breathing. The harder he tries to breathe, the more labored his breathing becomes. The more labored his breathing becomes, the more he experiences other physical symptoms: increased heart rate; feeling light-headed and dizzy; tingling and numbness in his toes, fingers, and scalp; pressure, even pain in his chest; and more. The more physical symptoms he experiences, the more scary thoughts start to intrude into his consciousness: *What if I'm having a heart attack, a stroke, or a sudden psychotic episode? What if I need emergency help?* and *How can I get out of here?* The more scary thoughts he experiences, the more afraid he becomes. And the more afraid he becomes, the more frantically he tries to fight off the impending panic and the harder he tries to "take a deep breath."

Owen was just tricked by his panic and worry. He felt the discomfort of short, shallow breathing and treated it like a danger, as if he were actually at risk of running out of air. He tried really hard to take a comfortable, full breath and ended up feeling worse, rather than better. He tried so hard that he had another panic attack.

If you've experienced panic attacks, you probably recognize this pattern. It typically starts with an initial symptom of anxiety—a scary what-if thought or a sudden uncomfortable physical sensation, like a racing heart or a shallow breath. Next thing you know, you're having more of that initial symptom, and other symptoms start to pile on as well. And you're trying, with all the reasoning power you possess, to calm yourself, without much success. You might find yourself having thoughts of various calamities—heart attack, stroke, insanity, nervous breakdown, fainting and collapsing, and so on. With each and every scary thought you experience, more physical symptoms jump into the fray, adding to your fears of a calamity and often motivating you to flee the scene. Once you've fled the scene, you feel better—but also worry more about the possibility of future episodes, and that's the road to a chronic anxiety disorder.

Each time this occurs, Owen gets more frustrated and fearful. He's been told many, many times to take a deep breath. He just tried it again, and it didn't work. In fact, it made his situation worse. Each time this happens to Owen, he tries even harder to take a deep breath. Each time, he gets the same miserable results.

How did he get tricked? When he felt short of breath, he tried to *inhale*. Inhaling under these circumstances *will* make the feelings worse. Here's where the Rule of Opposites can be so helpful.

What's the opposite of an inhale? An exhale. How ironic is that? He's been trying so hard to "take a deep breath," when all the time, he'd have better results if he'd give one away! That simple, opposite step—exhaling when your brain is screaming at you to "take a deep breath!"—is the best way to undo this trick and restore some comfort to your breathing.

Take a few moments now to try this breathing exercise. Read through it once first, and then go through the steps. Keep breathing your usual way while you figure out the instructions. Otherwise, you're likely to be holding your breath while you read, and that won't feel good!

Breathe Like a Baby

Before you start, put your left hand on your beltline and your right on your chest, on your sternum. Once you get good at this, you can stop using your hands. For now, use your hands to see what muscles you're using to breathe. What you want to find is that all the muscular work of your breathing is happening under your left hand, on your beltline. Use the muscles

Outsmart Your Anxious Brain

of your belly to do your breathing (this is what's often called "diaphragmatic breathing," but I prefer the simpler term "belly breathing"). The muscles of your chest needn't be involved in your breathing, and over time you will hopefully find those muscles doing less and less, and eventually, nothing.

1. Sigh gently, out through your mouth. (There's no need to fully empty your lungs. A sigh is a smaller version of a full exhale.) It's the kind of sigh you might make if you just heard something annoying. All those people who kept telling Owen to "take a deep breath"—they annoyed the heck out of him! Sigh like that. As you sigh, let your shoulders relax and let the muscles of your chest relax as well. When you're done with the sigh, close your mouth.

2. Pause. A couple of seconds is sufficient, but the precise timing isn't crucial. Do what feels comfortable.

3. Push the muscles of your belly out and forward while you inhale, slowly, through your nose. You're probably in the habit of holding your stomach in, but let go of that for now. Breathe like there's no one watching! The muscular expansion actually comes first and helps you take the inhale. When you've

taken in as much air as you can with your belly, stop. That's the end of the inhale. Don't throw your upper body into it.

4. Pause again.

5. Exhale, through your mouth, by pulling your belly muscles back in.

6. Pause one more time.

7. Repeat the inhale, and continue thereafter: exhale, pause, inhale, pause.

When you read the breathing instructions above, did you happen to have the thought, *That's the opposite of what I've been doing!?* That's a very common response and a good reminder of the Rule of Opposites.

Give belly breathing a try now. As you use the instructions, focus first on simply isolating your stomach muscles for a few seconds. As you get better at isolating and pushing out your stomach muscles, start pairing that with your breathing.

One common obstacle people experience is difficulty isolating the muscles of their stomach and pushing them out. They've been trained since their teenage years not to do

Outsmart Your Anxious Brain

that! Here are some exercises you can use to isolate those muscles and enhance your belly breathing technique.

- Interlace your fingers across your stomach and practice pushing your stomach out, then in. See if you can make your fingers spread apart a little as you expand your stomach. Practice this in a variety of postures—sitting, standing, and lying down.

- Lie on your back. Put a heavy book or other object on your chest to make it easier to focus on using your stomach muscles.

- Lie on your front, with a pillow beneath your stomach. Press your stomach against the pillow as you practice isolating your stomach muscles.

Another obstacle is simply force of habit. There's probably no habit you've repeated more often in your lifetime than breathing. Even as you read through the instructions and set out to breathe the way I describe, you might still find yourself breathing the old way at first. That's okay! Practice and repetition will help you.

Take your time and practice with these instructions, and I think you will start to see how to make this shift in your breathing. It's not new, after all. It's the way you used to breathe before you got caught up in anxiety patterns. If you want to see some world-class belly breathers, check out some infants or newborns. Their tummies go out as they inhale and come in as they exhale. That's how they breathe. They know nothing about chest breathing.

So this isn't about learning something entirely new and unknown. This is actually about getting back to a breathing style that you used to use all the time without even thinking about it.

Why do people start doing shallow chest breathing? Probably because, sometime in adolescence, they started paying attention to their body, wanting to have an attractive figure, and began feeling self-conscious about their belly. Then they started holding their belly in. Doing that makes belly breathing difficult, and so they started on the path of chest breathing. Ever hear this phrase, maybe from your mom, "Stomach in, chest out!"? She was trying to help you enhance your posture. But it made belly breathing more difficult.

As a group, people who struggle with anxiety disorders tend to have bad breathing technique. This is especially true for people with panic disorder, social anxiety disorder, and generalized anxiety disorder. They tend to inhale from their chest and often feel as though they're not getting a satisfactory breath. So they try harder to take a deep breath, only to find that this often aggravates, rather than solves, the problem. The irony of their "deep breath" in this situation is that there's nothing deep about it! It's a labored, shallow breath, one that comes from the chest rather than the belly. People often call it a deep breath, not because it's coming from a deep position, but because they put so much effort into it. And, of course, the reason they're putting so much muscular effort into breathing is because with chest breathing, they're breathing in a particularly ineffective and laborious way. It's the opposite of what newborns do, the opposite of what would be comfortable and efficient!

A picture is worth a thousand words, and a video, maybe a million! Here's a link to a video in which I demonstrate the breathing response: http://www.newharbinger.com/41993.

Practice Makes Better

Don't worry about doing it perfectly. We're built to breathe, and it doesn't require a lot of fine-tuning! However poorly you may have been breathing, you're still here, reading this book. Just modify your technique a little so you can feel a little more comfortable.

Once you have the hang of this, get some regular practice breathing this way so you can switch into belly breathing whenever it serves your purposes.

Here's what I suggest as a practice schedule. Get into the habit, during your day, of noticing your breath at the top of each hour—at noon, 1:00, 2:00, and so on. See how you're breathing, and then sigh, per the instructions above. Then continue with belly breathing for about one minute *while you go on doing whatever you were doing at the top of the hour.* Don't take time out to sit or lie down. Integrate the breathing into whatever you're doing at the time—walking, making a phone call, riding a bus, participating in a meeting, eating a sandwich, whatever. We want breathing to be portable and automatic, and this is a good way to accomplish that.

Do that for a day or two, and then check how often you're doing it. If you're doing the exercise at least eight or ten times a day, that's good. Keep doing that.

If, on the other hand, you find that you're not remembering to do it that often, then find some other ways to remind yourself. Tie a string around your finger or set your digital device to chime hourly. Put some colored stickers around your daily environment—office, home, car, whatever—and do the breathing exercise when you notice them. Or make it your habit to practice a minute of breathing in response to some frequently occurring events in your daily life. Do it whenever the phone rings, the baby cries, the dog barks, the horn honks, and so on. Get frequent practice with these brief, one-minute episodes, and let the habit grow.

One more thing. When you breathe this way, you're getting a larger volume of air than you do with those shallow chest breaths. So it will be good to breathe more slowly—a slower exhale, a longer pause, a slower inhale—than you've been used to. If you take these deeper breaths at the same rate as the shallow breaths, you will over-breathe. Nothing terrible about that, it's self-correcting, but I mention it because over-breathing often leads a person to yawn and also to feel light-headed. If you didn't know that, you might get fooled into thinking it meant something went wrong. It's harmless! It's just a reminder to slow down. If you experience either of those reactions, slow down your breathing a little.

Breathing, Panic, and Fainting

There's an interesting connection between the shallow breathing people experience as part of panic and high anxiety and the fear of fainting that's such a common part of a panic attack. Fainting is perhaps the most commonly feared outcome of a panic attack. Even people with no history of fainting as an adult—and that's the great majority of people who have panic attacks—feel certain symptoms of a panic attack and think that a faint is imminent. If they have no history with fainting, they don't know what a faint feels like, but this is the guess they make.

It's an understandable guess because they feel light-headed, maybe even dizzy. But these symptoms are typically caused by labored breathing, and as you get better at responding with belly breathing, you'll see that it relieves those symptoms as well.

What actually causes a person to faint? It's a sudden and significant drop in your blood pressure. When your blood pressure drops, the brain is the part of the body that has the most difficulty getting an adequate supply of freshly oxygenated blood because it's on the top. And yet the brain needs more freshly oxygenated blood than any other organ. How will your body solve this problem? Well, if you can't get enough blood up to the brain, fainting brings the brain down to the blood supply. This is why people typically regain consciousness quite quickly after fainting. Fainting isn't a catastrophe; it's the body's way of protecting you when your blood pressure falls too low.

But here's the $64 question: What's happening to your blood pressure during a panic attack? It's going up! Not a lot, but it's going up a little. Here's our friend the Rule of Opposites again. Your blood pressure is going in the *opposite direction* of what's needed to faint. There's hardly a time when it would be more difficult to faint than during a panic attack because your blood pressure is doing the opposite of what's required for fainting to occur!

That's why it's so extremely rare to faint during a panic attack. I've worked exclusively with clients with anxiety disorders over the past thirty years and have seen exactly five clients who did faint during a panic attack. All five of them had a relatively rare condition called postural orthostatic tachycardia syndrome (POTS), which causes unusual lightheadedness when you move quickly from lying down to standing up. A person with a severe case of POTS can faint during a panic attack and usually has a history of actually fainting. For these five clients with POTS, fainting was an actual problem to be managed, rather than a fear.

Much remains to be discovered about POTS. Estimates of prevalence vary, but it appears to involve considerably less than 1 percent of the population and is much more common among women of childbearing age. If you do have POTS, or an actual history of fainting episodes, find a qualified professional to help you manage your symptoms. On the other hand, if you frequently fear fainting without any adult history of actual faints, then what you probably have is a fear rather than a potential faint. Just thinking you'll win the lottery doesn't put a dollar in your pocket, and just thinking you'll faint doesn't knock you to the ground.

Blood phobia. One other note on the topic of fainting. People who have a blood phobia (the formal diagnostic term is blood-injury-injection phobia) can lose consciousness and faint when they see blood. I've worked with a few clients who had both a blood phobia and panic disorder. They would frequently faint when they saw blood but never faint while having a panic attack. They sometimes found themselves worrying about this, thinking that since they could faint at the sight of blood, then maybe they would also faint during a panic attack. They don't do that, and if you'd like to know why, here's a simple explanation of blood phobia.

For all of us, whenever we see blood, our blood pressure drops a little. This is a good thing because whenever you see blood, there's a chance it's yours! And if it is yours, a lowered blood pressure will enable you to clot faster, lose less blood, and have a lower risk of infection.

People with a blood phobia have too much of a good thing. Their blood pressure drops enough, when they see blood, to trigger a faint. The treatment for blood phobia is to learn how to manually raise your blood pressure (with muscular tension) in the target situations of giving a blood sample or donation, receiving an injection, attending surgery class in medical school, or wherever you may see blood. Blood phobia is more of a biological condition than a classic phobia.

Belly breathing and fear of public speaking. Belly breathing will also be very useful to people who fear public speaking: people who may experience a panic attack while addressing an audience. Panic attacks don't, and can't, cause the outcomes most people fear—death, insanity, loss of control, and so on. But if you're afraid of public speaking and experience labored, short, and shallow breathing or even hyperventilation during a presentation, that can make it difficult or impossible to continue talking because we make sounds by pushing air out from our lungs, which vibrates our vocal cords. If you experience this "breathlessness" while giving a presentation, it can bring your speaking to a halt until you correct that by shifting to belly breathing.

Is belly breathing a lifesaver? Does belly breathing save you from fainting or worse fates? Absolutely not! It just helps you moderate your symptoms so you are in a better position to stay in place and work with the fears you're having. Use belly breathing while you're having a panic attack so you can observe and defuse the symptoms rather than flee the scene.

Don't use belly breathing as a shield! Some anxiety specialists believe that it's better not to teach clients a breathing technique. They're concerned that the clients will think the breathing technique is saving them from a terrible fate and that this will make their panic and anxiety persist over time. In other words, they would be using belly breathing as a safety behavior to protect themselves, rather than a simple coping technique to help them stay in place and work with, rather than against, the panic. This can be a problem, but I believe clients are still better served by learning the belly breathing technique. If you see signs that you're relying on the breathing as a life-saving technique, or maybe becoming a little compulsive in working with your breathing, then periodically go back to the "bad, old" short and shallow breathing periodically, just enough to clarify that while it makes you feel uncomfortable, there's nothing dangerous about it.

Owen, who was experiencing a panic attack when we checked in on him at the beginning of this chapter, subsequently learned to use belly breathing. He was glad he did because it gave him a useful way of responding whenever he felt the gasping, short, and shallow breath that so often precipitates a full panic attack.

Several weeks after the panic attack he experienced in that staff meeting, he went back to the same room to attend another staff meeting with the same people. He really hoped he wouldn't have another one and found himself worrying about it the night before and all morning before the meeting started. Sure enough, he started having another panic attack as soon as the boss sat down and the door was closed. His chest felt tight and pressured, his heart seemed to race, he felt short of breath, and he thought he would faint. His brain started screaming at him, "Take a deep breath!"

And so he tried. Owen opened his mouth, tilted his head back, elevated his shoulders and chest, and struggled to inhale. It didn't feel good. Then he remembered the Rule of Opposites. He sighed and let the muscles of his upper body relax downward, with the sigh. He paused, then tentatively inhaled through his nose by pushing his stomach muscles out. It felt better! Owen felt encouraged to sit there and breathe this way while gradually turning his attention back to the meeting. He continued to notice some upsetting what-if thoughts for a while but kept bringing his attention back to the belly breathing and the discussion taking place around him. And so Owen sat through the entire meeting. He noticed the panic and accepted the symptoms as best he could, determined to let the panic leave the room before he did. That was the start of Owen's recovery from panic disorder.

The belly breathing didn't save him from fainting, dying, or any other calamity because he wasn't in danger, only afraid. Nor was it a silver bullet that prevented him from having any panic attacks. Instead, it gave him a tool he could use to stay in place and work *with* the panic symptoms, rather than against them. That made all the difference. Today there is nothing Owen avoids for fear of having a panic attack because he knows how to handle one if it arises. He has lost his fear of fear.

Sometimes people are pessimistic about their ability to benefit from belly breathing because they have tried so hard to "take a deep breath" in the past, only to feel worse for their efforts. The problem they had with all that instruction to "take a deep breath" was that no one had ever showed them *how* to take one. Now you know.

Thinking It Over

Feeling short of breath, with its attendant fears of fainting and dying, is perhaps the most universal of the panic symptoms. There's no danger, but plenty of discomfort, in this symptom. There's plenty of frustration and aggravation as well because when people try to take the deep breath they want, it often just brings more discomfort. The Rule of Opposites can guide you to start your breath with a sigh, rather than an inhale, and thereafter breathe with your belly rather than your chest.

In the next chapter, we'll look at how people get tricked into avoiding the things they fear, how that makes their fears worse rather than better, and how they can counter this trick. But before you start the next chapter, maybe take a few minutes to get started with your breathing practice.

Chapter 4

Practice, Don't Protect

When you're afraid of something—an object or living creature, a place or situation, or an activity—there's a natural tendency to avoid it.

This is usually a good thing. Fear alerts us to potential dangers in our environment. It gives us the signal, the motivation, and the energy to protect ourselves, typically with fight or flight responses. When we feel fear because we smell smoke in a theater or notice a dog growling and showing signs of aggression, that fear is a useful and timely signal of danger. It tells us, "Protect yourself or you might get hurt." That's the kind of signal that helps keep us safe.

But we can also become afraid when we're not in any danger, and that's the tricky part. We can become afraid in response to unpleasant thoughts, emotions, and physical sensations within us, rather than in response to dangerous objects and events in the environment. That's how people with fears and phobias get tricked into avoiding and fleeing ordinary activities, objects, and locations that aren't particularly dangerous.

When you get tricked into avoiding something that's not dangerous, you get the immediate, short-term benefit of a reduction in fear. But in the long term, you become more afraid of the object or situation that you avoid. You're trading away your long-term freedom of action for a few moments of temporary comfort, and it's a very bad trade. You give away a lot and get very little in return.

The best way to counter that trick and obtain a better trade is to practice with, rather than protect yourself against, the activities, objects, and locations that trigger those fears.

When you experience a moment of high anxiety—be it a panic attack, a scary obsessive thought, a sudden fear of social rejection, a concern about insanity—it's like the opening scene of your own private scary movie. The fact that the movie is playing in the theater of your mind, rather than in a movie theater, doesn't make any difference. We're just as affected by our internal thoughts, emotions, and physical sensations as we are by objects and events in the world around us—maybe even more affected. And simply knowing "It's only a movie!" doesn't prevent you from feeling afraid.

You get fooled by the worry trick when you treat all fears as if they were accurate and timely warnings of danger, requiring fight or flight responses. This is why people come to my office: they're experiencing fears that don't offer them any useful signal of danger. They know their fear isn't helpful or realistic, but they don't know how to stop it from interfering in their daily lives.

Your best way to know which fears to take seriously and which to disregard is to rely on your experience. Whether you're afraid of dogs, flying, highway driving, mistakenly leaving your door unlocked or your stove on, public speaking, or meeting strangers—whatever you fear—your past experience with those objects and activities will be your best guide.

Is Avoidance a Problem for You?

Let's get started with this exercise by answering these questions in your notebook.

1. What triggers your fear? It might be something in the world around you: an object, animal, or person; attending an event; participating in an activity; or encountering a distressing situation. Or it might be something within you: a thought, a physical sensation, or an emotion.

2. When you meet the object, person, or animal; participate in the event or activity; encounter the situation; or experience the thought, sensation, or emotion and then become afraid, what are you

afraid that the external situation or your internal reaction will do to you?

3. Has it ever done that to you? (yes or no)

If your answer to question 3 is yes, that would indicate there's some danger associated with your fear or there has been at some point in your life. For instance, many adults have a history of being bitten by a dog when they were a child, but they are now much less likely to be victimized by a dog as an adult. A yes answer to this question doesn't necessarily mean you face danger now, but this type of situation would merit review with a professional therapist if you find it troublesome.

Maybe your answer isn't simply yes or no but something like one of these:

- Not yet, but what if it does?

- Not so far, but I've just been lucky!

- No, because I had my medication (or my cell phone, water bottle, support person, emotional support animal, or some other aid) to help me.

If that's the case, then you may be getting tricked into giving more credibility and attention to your thoughts and fears than your actual experience. Chapters 5 through 7 will describe the various ways people get tricked this way and what you can do about it.

If your answer is a simple no, however, that neither your fear nor your feared object has ever done anything harmful to you then that indicates you know you're up against discomfort, rather than danger. This is a situation in which you can make immediate use of the Rule of Opposites.

What's the opposite of avoidance? It's to approach and experience the thing you've been avoiding. This is what psychologists usually call "exposure." I'm going to call it "practice." If you've been avoiding elevators, it's practice with elevators. If you've been avoiding dogs, it's dogs, and if you've been avoiding flying, you guessed it…flying. The opposite of phobic avoidance is practice with the situation, object, or activity you fear.

Practice Feeling Afraid

When people come to my office, they usually arrive with the hope that I will show them how to be unafraid of the airplane, the dog, the public speaking, or whatever they fear. They wish that *first* they'll lose their fear, and *then* they'll go deal with the situation or object that they used to fear.

You can do both: lose your fear and deal with the situations you fear. But usually not in that order. People learn to be less afraid on the airplane, for the fearful flyer; with the dog, for the dog phobic; driving on the highway, for people who fear that; and so on.

To help you understand this, I need to tell you a little about the brain. When we think about our brain, we usually just think of the part that engages in conscious thought and deliberation (the cerebral cortex). But there are many other parts of the brain, each with its own function, and most of those parts operate outside our conscious awareness. We can't be aware of the functioning of our cerebellum, for instance. The cerebellum maintains our physical balance, and it does so outside of our conscious awareness. We can observe the results of its functioning only in the fact that we stand up rather than fall down.

There are other parts of the brain that are involved in detecting danger. The amygdala, in particular, is heavily involved in strong emotional arousal and fight-or-flight responses. The amygdala is our front line of defense, the part of the brain most immediately tasked with the job of keeping us safe and alive.

The amygdala, like the cerebellum, operates outside of our conscious awareness. This is what enables it to respond so rapidly when it detects an emergency. The part of your brain that you probably think of as "you"—your cerebral cortex—can't directly reason with, or override, your amygdala. In fact, when your amygdala gets activated and declares an emergency, your cerebral cortex is essentially silenced and removed from the action until the crisis has passed.[4]

This is why an elevator-phobic may recognize that her fears are terribly exaggerated and yet be completely unable to talk herself out of her fear. It's the same with a dog-phobic, a flying-phobic, a person with contamination fears, a social-phobic, and so on. The essence of an anxiety disorder is that people become afraid in the absence of danger. Even when they know that, they can't talk themselves out of their fear!

And, unfortunately, when they fail to talk themselves out of their fear, they tend to blame themselves. They often attribute this to their being too weak, too cowardly, too stupid, or defective somehow. But the reason they can't talk themselves out of their fear has more to do with how the brain is structured than their personal characteristics. Specifically, it's because our brains are wired to allow the amygdala to override, and even silence, the input of the cerebral cortex when responding to an apparent crisis. During such a time, we can literally act without conscious thought.

This is usually a good thing because the amygdala works much faster than the cerebral cortex, and that's what you want in an emergency. The reason you can't simply talk yourself out of your fears, even the ones you can recognize are exaggerated and unrealistic, is that the amygdala isn't accepting any calls from the cerebral cortex. It's too busy dealing with possible emergencies!

You can't redirect your amygdala just by talking to it, but you can retrain it. If you're going to retrain your amygdala, here's one more fact you need to know: the amygdala "learns" and creates new memories only when it's activated. Know what I mean by "activated"? It's when you're afraid and your amygdala is trying so hard to protect you. So a person who fears elevators and wants to train his amygdala to be less fearful of riding in them will need to follow these key steps:

1. Enter an elevator.

2. Feel afraid as his amygdala goes on full alert, activating its "elevator = bad" association and filling him with fear.

3. Ride the elevator long enough to give his amygdala time to notice that nothing bad happens.

4. Leave after his amygdala has settled down and created a new memory that says elevators are sometimes okay.

5. Repeat as necessary, in a variety of elevators, to strengthen the "elevator = okay" learning until it becomes the dominant association your amygdala has about elevators.

If you're unhappy with how your amygdala handles encounters with dogs or airplanes, you can change that, but not by arguing with your amygdala. If you're unhappy with how your biceps look, you can change that, but not by arguing with your biceps. Your biceps won't listen to you any more than your amygdala will. You can change your biceps by putting them through the right kind of exercise to change them. And so it is with the amygdala. You can retrain it by putting it through the right kind of exercises.

The point of exposure practice isn't to show up and not feel afraid. The point of practice is to show up, feel afraid, and hang out with it to give it time to diminish. Avoidance maintains and builds fears, and practice reduces them. Practice with your fears is the way you can retrain your amygdala and gradually reduce your fear. That's what exposure practice is all about. It's not about getting tougher or braver or smarter. It's about retraining your amygdala.

Right now you might be wondering how you can stay in place and patiently allow yourself to feel afraid. Here's how.

AWARE Steps

This is a five-step guide you can use to conduct yourself during a practice session or any experience of high anxiety.[5]

Accept

When you notice that you're feeling afraid, you probably want to resist and stop feeling that way. Of course! You don't want these symptoms, you don't deserve them, and they don't feel good. If you could simply toss them aside, the way you might change your clothes after getting caught in a downpour, that would be helpful. But you can't. When you try, you're likely to get caught up in a struggle against your own thoughts, emotions, physical sensations, and automatic responses. The result of this struggle will be more, not less, anxiety. Resistance is not only futile—it makes you feel worse! And the opposite of resistance is…acceptance.

So take the counterintuitive choice, go in the opposite direction, and allow yourself, as passively as possible, to experience and accept the symptoms while you wait for them to pass. Why would you do this? Two reasons. First, because it will probably allow the symptoms to fade and pass more quickly than when you oppose them. And second, because this response will help you regain your long-term freedom to ride elevators, tolerate dogs, give presentations at your school or church, fly in airplanes, or whatever it is that you want to be able to do.

How does this compare with how you usually react when you become anxious? If you're like most people, it's probably the *opposite* of how you usually react.

Watch

Watch what? Watch yourself. Watch the symptoms you experience and your instinctive urge to respond immediately. Use the self-observational journal templates (download them at http://www.newharbinger.com/41993) to notice and record your observations of the anxiety symptoms. Notice any urges to flee or to distract yourself and record them as well. This will help you get more into the role of observer. The more firmly you occupy the role of observer, the less likely you are to get tricked by your anxiety.

How does this compare with your usual reaction?

Act

Now, having gone through the first two steps of accept and watch, this might be a good time to take some action. Those first two steps function like the old adage of "count to ten before you get mad," buying yourself some time in order to choose a truly useful course of action.

What action should you choose? It depends on what you think your job is when you're responding to an episode of high anxiety. What's your job when you're having a panic attack, a moment of high worry, or an obsessive thought that keeps hammering at you to respond with a ritual? If I could somehow eavesdrop on your thoughts at such a moment, what would I hear you telling yourself to do?

Most people suppose that it's their job to stop the anxiety. It's not.

It's not your job to stop the anxiety because every anxiety episode ends no matter what you do. When you do everything the most cogent way possible to bring it to an end, it ends. When you do everything in the most unhelpful way possible—fighting and fleeing the source of the anxiety—that episode also ends. Every anxiety episode ends no matter what you do.

Have you ever had an anxiety episode that didn't end? I've asked this question of a lot of people, and I'm going to assume your answer is the same as theirs. No, you never had an episode that didn't end because they all end, no matter how you react. They probably don't all end as quickly as you would like, but that's a different kind of problem, requiring a different kind of solution.

So it's not your job to make the episode end. What is your job during an anxiety episode? It's much more modest: to see if you can feel a little more comfortable, a little less upset, while waiting for it to end. And if you can't feel any more comfortable, then your job is simply to follow these steps and wait for it to end. Because they all end. And the more you can fit yourself into this role—to accept the temporary anxiety and wait, as passively as possible, for it to end—the sooner it will end.

With that job in mind—waiting for it to end—what are some actions you can take in this step, while you're waiting?

If you're willing to hang out and do nothing, that works because nothing is really required. The episode will end on its own. But that might be expecting too much of yourself, at least in the early stages of your recovery work. You might prefer to do something, and that's understandable. Perhaps later, after you've made some progress, you can start letting go of any responses in this step. For now, the best responses will be relatively modest ones because nothing big is required here, and less will get you more. The best responses will also incorporate the Rule of Opposites. Here are some you can use.

1. The single action most likely to be helpful is belly breathing, especially when you're feeling strong physical symptoms of anxiety in your upper body. It is also quite helpful with the confusion and desperation that accompany the belief that you are running out of air. Belly breathing will help you breathe more comfortably as you stay in place and give the symptoms a chance to decline and pass.

2. You may also find it helpful to have a different way of responding to those anxiety-provoking what-if thoughts that are so often part of an anxiety episode.

If you're like most anxiety sufferers, you probably resist those thoughts in some way. Maybe you argue with them, trying to disprove them. Maybe you try to distract yourself and change the subject. Maybe you try thought stopping. These responses don't usually help much. What you resist, persists.

How many times have family and friends tried to help you out of an anxiety episode by telling you to "calm down"? Or by pointing out that your fears seem exaggerated or unrealistic or unlikely? Or by telling you to "stop thinking about it"?

Not only are those responses usually unhelpful, they're also usually pretty annoying! And you know what? They won't work any better when you use them on yourself. What would be the opposite of those responses? The opposite of resisting your fearful thoughts would be to agree and play with them: literally to humor your anxious thoughts. That will be the topic of chapter 6.

How does this step compare with how you usually react?

Repeat

R stands for repeat. It's here to remind you that you might start feeling better as you use the AWARE steps and then feel another upsurge in anxiety. R is here to remind you that that's okay, you might experience that, and if you do, just run through the steps again. Take it from the top, as often as you need. If we didn't have the R here, you might suppose something had gone wrong, that the steps weren't working. Keep in mind that your job is to see if you can feel a little more comfortable while waiting for the episode to end, and use the R step in that spirit.

How does this step compare with what you usually do?

End

This last step is another reminder that the anxiety episode will end, all on its own, no matter what you do. The end of an anxiety episode is just as much a part of an anxiety episode as is the start of one. It comes with the package. It's not something you have to supply.

This is worth emphasizing because all too often, the thoughts of an anxiety sufferer are filled with worries about it ending, such as:

- *When will it end?*

- *What if it doesn't end?*

- *How can I make it end?*

It's not your job to make it end, and that's very much worth remembering.

Thinking It Over

It's a natural response to avoid what seems fearful, but when it becomes habitual, it contributes to the maintenance of anxiety disorders. Working "with" rather than against the signs and symptoms of anxiety can help you move in a better direction. The AWARE steps are a helpful guide to follow when you're looking to counter the avoidant urge.

The next chapter will look at how you can get better at noticing the trick of what-if thoughts and begin to take those thoughts less seriously.

Chapter 5

Catch Worry in the Act

If you who struggle with chronic worry, you are often flooded with what-if thoughts about bad events that could possibly happen in the future. These what-if thoughts are the bait that lures you into obsessing about a bad event that, while it's unlikely to happen, is possible...because nothing is truly impossible! Once you get tricked into taking the bait, you're hooked—maybe for a few minutes, maybe for a few hours, maybe for the entire morning—as you work that worrisome thought for all it's worth. Sooner or later, that episode of worry ends, but it feels lousy while it lasts, and you're strengthening a worry habit that keeps recurring.

These what-if thoughts are like the bait on a fisherman's line. A fish that fails to notice the slight glimmer of a silver hook behind the tasty-looking worm is likely to bite down on the hook, and now it's got a much bigger problem than being hungry. Fish that manage to learn to discriminate between baited hooks and actual food are more likely to enjoy a long life. It's not the same life-or-death choice for you. But you can learn to recognize the bait of what-if thoughts and train yourself to stand down, rather than get engaged in a mental struggle with the hypothetical bad event it pretends to predict. That's the path to worrying less and enjoying life more for people who have become mired in a pattern of chronic worry.

Worry tricks you, and plays you for a sucker, the same way that the fisherman and his worm trick the fish. It sneaks in the door with its message of menace and gets you engaged in worry before you have a chance to realize you're being tricked. It's a powerful, effective trick that unfortunately ensnares millions of good, competent, intelligent, and worthwhile people. Fortunately, almost all of this chronic worry comes preannounced by those two words—"What if?"—and you can use those words to help direct you back to what's more important in life than all this repetitive worrying.

How a Successful Guy Keeps Getting Hooked on Worry

Chris, a successful business executive in his early thirties, has a performance review in two weeks with his boss. He's been with his firm for three years and has been successful and well regarded during that time. His first two reviews went very well. But each year, as the date for his annual review

Outsmart Your Anxious Brain

approaches, he becomes quite anxious about it, and this year is no exception.

His wife, Carol, recognizes the pattern. Chris frequently mentions his concerns over breakfast. "What if they're not so happy with me this year?" She reminds him that he said the same thing last year, but that doesn't reassure him. "What if this is the year the boss comes down on me?" Carol points out that he's had three very good years with the company. "Nothing lasts forever," he replies. "Maybe I should update my résumé. What if I'm suddenly without a job?" "You'll do fine," his wife says, hoping to silence his fears. Chris does get silent, but that's because he suspects she's just telling him what he wants to hear. She reminds him that he went through a similar period of worry about not finding a job when he first entered the job market—"What if I can't find a job?"—but that doesn't comfort him either.

Chris Argues with Himself

Chris has gotten caught up in an argument with his worry. He keeps experiencing unwanted, fearful what-if thoughts that scare and upset him. Chris takes the content of these thoughts seriously, as if they were an important warning of future trouble. He tries many things to win the argument and bring the worry to an end. He tries to:

- distract himself

- suppress the thoughts

- disprove the thoughts

- replace the thoughts with something more positive

- get reassurance from his wife

- persuade himself that all will be well.

Chris doesn't recognize that, in arguing with his thoughts, he is actually arguing with himself. There is no contest on the planet more evenly matched than a person arguing with himself. This is a match that can last a long time!

Carol gets stuck as well as she tries to reassure him that he won't get fired because she can't really prove that either. It's always possible to get fired or experience some negative event in the future. Trying to convince yourself, or someone else, that a bad event just can't happen is more likely to prolong the arguing than to soothe the worry. Neither Chris nor Carol makes any progress in this conversation because getting fired isn't the problem right now. Getting tricked into worrying about being fired—that's the problem!

Worry Isn't About Future Failures;
It's About Feeling Nervous Now

There are several ways you can experience nervousness. Physical sensations, such as sweaty palms and changes in heart rate, are one way. Behaviors, such as nail-biting, leg-jiggling, and other forms of restlessness, are another. And worrisome thoughts, most notably what-if thoughts of future possible catastrophes, are another. Thoughts are the type of nervous symptom that people often have the most trouble recognizing and handling.

It's probably easy for you to recognize nail-biting or some other uncomfortable feeling, like restlessness or boredom, as a sign of nervousness. You're unlikely to think that you're biting your nails because you're hungry or because you have a nutritional deficiency. It's probably also easy for you to recognize jiggling your foot or leg as a sign of nervousness. You probably don't think it's because you want to play Hacky Sack. It's the same with sweaty palms during a presentation. You probably don't think it means you have too much water in your body. You probably recognize it as a sign of nervousness.

But when Chris has these what-if thoughts about getting a poor job evaluation, and even losing his job, he reacts as if these thoughts were valid warnings of upcoming job trouble.

For some people, in some situations, they could be. But Chris has a good work history and a good relationship with his boss and coworkers. His thought, *What if I get a poor job evaluation?* isn't a valid warning of a poor job evaluation in the future. It's a symptom of nervousness now. It means the same thing as sweaty palms or nail-biting. Chris doesn't have a future problem that he's worrying about—he has the present problem of worrying.

Worry sneaks up on us, approaching from the back of our mind, so we don't even notice it's tricked us again. It's subliminal. That makes us easier to get tricked. The first step in overcoming this problem is to more clearly see how the worry thought works.

Diagram the Worry Sentence

The typical worry thought has two parts, and looks like this:

What if…[*catastrophe clause*]?

What goes in the catastrophe clause? Anything bad that isn't happening right now. This is the "Mad Libs" of chronic worry. You can insert any bad thing in the catastrophe clause, and the sentence will work, so long as the bad thing isn't occurring at the moment.

What if…I have cancer?

What if…my spouse leaves me?

What if…she takes all our money?

What if…she leaves the twins?

Most people who struggle with worry don't notice the what-if words. They just notice the catastrophe clause because it sounds so threatening and terrible. Let's take a closer look at how the what-if clause works in the worry sentence.

In the game of Mad Libs, participants are invited to fill in blank spaces in sentences with various words—adjectives, personal pronouns, colors, and so forth—and hopefully create a humorous or nonsensical story that others at the party will enjoy.

The what-if clause invites you to do something similar but without much prospect of enjoyment. Here is the invitation: think of something bad that isn't happening right now…and pretend that it is! That's what "What if?" really means: "Let's pretend something bad!"

This is why people can get so upset, so anxious, feel sick to their stomach, experience their heart racing, and feel so distraught in response to a thought: they're literally imagining a world in which that awful thing is happening or about to happen. They're pretending that it will happen and imagining how that will feel. It's like their own private movie theater in their mind, one that only shows horror films!

If you can get better at noticing the what-if clause in your thoughts, it might help you avoid taking the catastrophe clause so seriously. The what-if clause is the best reminder you will get that you don't have a problem right now.

Consider a person with a severe dog phobia who worries constantly about a dog bite. She worries when she's safely locked in her home because she knows she has to go outside the next day. She worries when she's at work on the twentieth floor of an exclusive office building because she knows she has to leave to go home. She has worrisome dreams about a dog biting her, even as she sleeps soundly in her locked and gated home. When is the only time she's guaranteed to not be worrying about a dog biting her?

When a dog is biting her! She's too busy defending herself then—looking for a stick, yelling for help, climbing a fence, doing whatever she can do to protect herself. The presence of these provocative what-if questions is the best reminder she can have that the chips are not down at that moment. If the chips were down, she'd be fending off the dog, not wrestling with thoughts. Wrestling with what-if thoughts is a leisure-time activity. We don't do it when the chips are down!

It will be so valuable for you to get better at catching your what-if thoughts in the act. The what-if clause is your

Outsmart Your Anxious Brain

last and best chance to get off on the right foot, rather than taking the bait and becoming embroiled in an argument with yourself about the content of the catastrophe clause. You can train yourself to get better at noticing the what-if thoughts, and that will help you sidestep the arguments with yourself.

Here's how you can start doing that.

Observing Your What-If Thoughts

Get yourself some boxes of Tic Tacs, or any mint that comes in a specific quantity to the box or bottle. Tic Tacs come in boxes of sixty. Get into this habit: carry your box of Tic Tacs everywhere you go. Every time you notice yourself thinking (or saying) the words "what if," open your box and take one out. You can eat it if you like or flick it into the trash if you don't. Use the Tic Tacs as a simple way to keep count of how many times a day or week you experience a what-if thought.

This is an odd little exercise, sure enough, but I encourage you to do it regularly for a couple of weeks and periodically after that to maintain the habit. Be less concerned with the actual number (which, by the way, will probably be higher than you expect) than with creating the habit of counting. (And if you prefer using a clicker, or some other method of counting, that's okay too.) The habit of counting will help you get better at catching yourself in the act of having this thought. This way, you can make some choices about how to respond to the thought, rather than having it influence your mood and choices without you even noticing. This is an example of what's meant by the phrase "making the unconscious conscious."

Here's something that probably happened to you if you were home having dinner in the United States circa 2002, before there was a "do not call" law. The phone rang, and when you answered, the caller said, "Hello, I have some free magazines to give you!" If you took that to mean that some generous person was sending you a gift, you probably ended up buying stuff that you didn't really need. If, instead, you recognized it as a sales call from a telemarketer and responded accordingly, you probably came out of that all right.

The effect this call had on you depended on whether you thought the call was a gift or an attempt to sell you something. The effect the what-if thoughts have on you depend on whether you think they're an important warning about the future or just another instance of feeling nervous in the present moment. That's why it's so useful to get in the habit of clearly noticing the what-if clause before your attention races ahead to the inflammatory catastrophe clause.

Once you've been working with the Tic Tacs for a couple of days, add this: pick a trusted person with whom you're in frequent contact, maybe a spouse or a good friend, someone

Outsmart Your Anxious Brain

you know to firmly have your best interests at heart. Explain to that person what you're doing with what-if thoughts. Ask that person to notice when you say, "What if?" in conversation with them and to respond with some simple gesture to point that out to you. They could briefly point an index finger at you or make a hitchhiking gesture with their thumb, anything that serves to point out to you that you just said "What if?". They can do something similar when you're talking on the phone, texting, or e-mailing—maybe use a particular emoji or phrase to briefly help you catch yourself in the act.

Once you're better at catching yourself in the act of a what-if thought, you'll be in a much better position to respond to worrisome thoughts in a more useful way.

Some people who struggle with chronic worry know all too well that the content of the "catastrophe clause" in their worrisome thoughts is unrealistic and exaggerated. All they have to do is catch themselves in the act of having a what-if thought, and they can recognize that once again, they're hearing the noisy nonsense of repetitive, exaggerated worry. They might not find it so easy to dismiss or silence the thoughts but they can recognize that the thought itself is simply a symptom of nervousness, rather than an indication of an actual threat. It's literally a "thought symptom," and it means the same as a physical symptom, such as sweaty palms—it means you're nervous. If you're one of those people, you just need different ways of responding to the thought symptom, and you can skip over this next section if you like.

What If Your Worries Seem Realistic?

Others, though, report that their what-if worries focus on more realistic concerns. They think there may be a valid, realistic warning in their thoughts, and they get caught up in struggling with them. Not only are they unable to dismiss the worrisome thoughts, but they don't think they should because they believe the worries predict bad possibilities that are quite likely. They think that worries prepare them for future bad events.

This may include worries such as:

- *What if we can't find a buyer for our home?* (after six months on the market with few showings and no offers)

- *What if my elderly parent dies?* (when the parent is realistically approaching the end of life)

- *What if my son can't get into any colleges he wants?* (when the son actually has a low grade-point average)

- *What if I lose my job?* (when my company is having financial troubles and my last two performance evaluations have been ranked "unsatisfactory")

The Two-Part Test

When you think there might be a useful signal in your worry content, use this two-part question to evaluate it.

1. Does the problem I'm worrying about exist in the world around me now, the world outside of my mind and imagination?

2. If it does, is there anything I can do to change it now?

If you get two yes answers to these questions, then maybe worry isn't your main problem. The two yes answers would indicate that you have a worry about an actual problem that exists now, outside of your mind, a problem you can do something about. That's what ordinary worry is for, to remind you to take action when you can, and that's probably what you need to do.

People who find evidence of a problem in the world around them—their son is having trouble getting into college, an aged parent is likely to die in the near future, or their job is at risk—will be better served by taking action to avoid or prepare for that problem than they would be struggling with the worry. If the worry persists after they have taken whatever actions are available to them and there's no longer any useful information being conveyed by the thought, then they could simply notice the thought and respond in the manner described in this chapter and the next.

But if you get any other combination of answers—a no to the first question, a yes and a no, or answers like *what if, couldn't it happen, imagine that, I suppose*—then you don't have a problem you're worrying about; you have the problem of worrying.

If Chris were to apply this test to his worries about his upcoming job evaluation, he would likely get a no to the first question. There doesn't appear to be anything going on in the world around him that is problematic. The only sign of "trouble" is the nervous thoughts that he experiences within his own mind. And since there isn't a problem in the world around him, there is nothing "out there" he can change.

If that's what you have—worrisome thought symptoms, rather than an actual problem in the external world that you need to solve—then it will be helpful to accept and humor those thoughts, rather than get tricked into taking the content seriously.

If you have an actual problem out there in the world around you and you've already done whatever you can do about it, well then, there's no longer any useful signal in your worry thought, and you can treat it the same way. That thought is like a duplicate copy of an e-mail that you already responded to. It no longer has any important information you can use.

Thinking It Over

What-if thoughts can easily trick you into feeling as though bad things are happening when you're only having thoughts of bad things running through your mind. If you take the bait of these thoughts and argue with them, this will fuel the worry habit.

Use the Tic Tacs and other aids to get better at detecting the trick in your own worrisome thoughts. When you are better able to notice the bait of what-if thoughts, you'll be in a better position to respond in a different manner.

The next chapter will show you a variety of ways to respond differently once you've noticed the what-if bait.

Chapter 6

Humor Your Worries

It's all too easy to get tricked into taking the content of the what-if thoughts seriously. Even if you recognized the call from the telemarketer as a sales call, that wouldn't help much if you got into an angry argument with him, tried to show him the error of his ways, or treated the call seriously in any way at all. Unfortunately, that's what most people do. They take the content of the worry seriously. Even when they recognize that the thoughts are unreasonable and unlikely, they often argue with them and feel worse for the effort.

Taking the content of these what-if thoughts seriously causes problems...and so an effective counter might be to take these thoughts more lightly and respond to the anxiety they offer with humor.

Does it worry you to think about humoring your worries? Are you concerned that you'll overlook some important warning? That's what the Two-Part Test is for.

1. Does the problem exist now, in the world around me?

2. If it does, is there anything I can do to change it now?

I'm going to suppose you've already evaluated your worrisome thoughts with the Two-Part Test and want to respond differently the next time your what-if thoughts bait you. How can you respond differently?

Muhammad Ali was perhaps the most famous boxer in the history of the sport. After he won the world heavyweight title the second time in 1974, he attributed his victory against a much younger, larger, and stronger fighter to his "rope-a-dope" technique. Rope-a-dope, he explained, consisted of him leaning back against the ropes, dodging and absorbing his opponent's punches until his opponent had punched himself out and was too tired to fight well. And the "dope," Ali explained, was the opponent who followed him to the ropes and did all that fruitless punching.

When it comes to responding to what-if thoughts, don't be that dope! The content of those what-if thoughts is generally for suckers. When you're frequently being bothered and interrupted by what-if thoughts of problems that either don't exist now or can't be changed if they do, then you're being heckled, yes heckled, by your own worry thoughts.

What's the best way to handle heckling? A performer who's being heckled might be tempted to take off his jacket and rush into the audience for a fistfight with the heckler, but that's not going to help him perform his show. Nor will it help to try to ignore the heckling because he's still hearing it, and the audience knows that. Probably the best way for a performer to respond to heckling is to work that heckling into his act. That's an effective way to disarm heckling.

Arguing with your worries usually makes things worse. The opposite of arguing is humoring, agreeing with, and playing with the worries. Here are some ways you can do that.

Paradoxical Repetition

First, pick a time and place where you can have complete privacy, without the need to be responsive to others, including children, dogs, the phone or doorbell, and so on. You might need fifteen to thirty minutes for this task.

Select a topic you often worry about, one that fails the Two-Part Test: either it doesn't describe a problem that actually exists in the world outside your mind right now or, if it does, there isn't anything you can possibly do to change it now.

Next, create a worry sentence of about twenty words, one that incorporates all the worst fears you have about this topic. Include your fears about it today, and also imagine what it would be like to look back on your life in old age, as you contemplate a life ruined and laid waste by this hypothetical problem.

Since the first two words will be what-if, you have about eighteen words to work with. Take a few minutes now to create a powerful expression of this worry. This will probably be unpleasant! Don't let that stop you; the discomfort will pass.

Once you have your worry sentence, sit or stand in front of a mirror, and repeat your worry out loud twenty-five times, slowly and methodically. The point of this is to be aware of your worry sentence in as many sensory channels as possible. People usually worry while they're engaged in other activities, while they're multitasking. They worry while they're driving, eating, taking a shower, and more. Multitasking while you're worrying makes it hard to observe your worries, making it more likely that you'll get tricked. Focus on your worries when you do this to ensure that you're not multitasking.

Don't keep count in your head. Rather, use one of these two methods for counting: Make twenty-five marks on a piece of paper and cross one out with each repetition, or put twenty-five coins on a table and move them from one side to the other, one with reach repetition.

Go ahead and create your worry sentence now. Don't hold back by confining yourself to moderately unpleasant material in creating this worry sentence. Put as much of the distress, despair, and anxiety in it as you can. This exercise works best when you fill your sentence with the core ideas of your most unpleasant and disturbing worry content.

When you have a good worry sentence, go ahead and do the twenty-five repetitions out loud, preferably before you read any further.

All done repeating? How did the emotional impact of the last repetition compare with the emotional impact of the first repetition?

Most people expect that the repetition of this unpleasant worrisome thought will be very upsetting and that their upset will grow as they continue to repeat it. This is why people so frequently turn to distraction, figuring that the way to feel better is to stop having the worrisome thoughts.

However, most people find that the repetition drains the upsetting power from the worry sentence. By the time they finish the twenty-fifth repetition, it's no longer nearly as upsetting as it was on the first repetition. It's been reduced to just a sound. They discover that exposure methods don't just work for objects and activities, like animals and public speaking. Exposure also works well with worrisome thoughts!

That was what Chris found when he used this technique. He created this sentence: "What if my boss fires me, I never work again, my wife leaves me, I never see my kids, and I die young, drunk, and destitute?"

It certainly wasn't easy or comfortable to create this thought, and the first couple of repetitions felt terrible. It's full of terrible ideas, right? And yet Chris found that the more he repeated it, the more relaxed he felt. He was grinning by the eighth repetition, and by the twenty-fifth time, the sentence seemed meaningless. And of course, when Chris had his review, it was a lot like his previous reviews and nothing like his anticipated version.

Give this a try. If you have a reaction like Chris did, then consider the irony of this situation. People try so hard to banish an upsetting what-if thought from their mind, yet get more relief from indulging the thought in twenty-five repetitions!

Worry in a Foreign Language

If you happen to be bilingual, it will probably help to do your worrying in your weaker language. Each time you notice the what-if thoughts or find yourself embroiled in worrying about them, switch to the language in which you're less fluent, and worry in that one.

And if you're not bilingual? This was Chris's concern. He only had a couple of years of high school French. He worried he wasn't fluent enough to worry well in French! But how good do you have to be? It's only worry thoughts! Consult a dictionary if you feel the need (How do you say "choke to death" in German?), or blend what little you know with English and speak in Spanglish or Frenglish. Don't know any foreign languages at all? Use pig Latin!

Make a Poem Out of Your Worry Content

Many of my clients have found it especially helpful to create a simple haiku of their worries: three lines of unrhymed verse in which the first line has five syllables, the second has seven, and the third has five. See if you can include some element of surprise or irony in the final line (but don't worry about it if you can't!).

Here's a haiku from Chris:

My boss will fire me
Lose home, wife, kids, all is lost
Can I wash your car?

If a haiku seems too exotic, how about a limerick? It's a humorous poem with five lines. The first, second, and fifth lines have seven to ten syllables while rhyming with each other and having the same verbal rhythm. The third and fourth lines have five to seven syllables while rhyming with each other and having the same rhythm. Here's one from a (former) fearful flyer.

I'm going to get on that plane
Even though it will drive me insane

I'll kick down the door
Get thrown to the floor
And everyone will soon know my name

Make a Song Out of Your Worry Content

Create some lyrics that simply state the most fearful and outlandish concerns you hear in your worries. Fit them into simple popular tunes that you can sing silently or, better yet, out loud. The purpose of these songs is not to silence or banish your worrisome thoughts. Rather, it's to give them room, to air them out and accept them in a playful way.

If you'd like to hear a couple of my songs about panic attacks, they're available at http://www.newharbinger.com /41993.

Walk in Worry Shoes

Here is an interesting experiment. Take a walk for somewhere between two and five minutes. Walking around your block might be ideal, if the weather's good, but you can also walk around in your basement. While you're walking, keep this thought in mind: *I can't move; my legs are broken.* It's obviously untrue, but that's okay; this is an experiment.

When you're done, consider these questions:

- How do you feel as you walk around with this thought in your mind?

- What attitude do you have toward the thought as you walk around?

Think of other times when you've had an untrue or exaggerated worrisome thought in your mind. How did you feel with that thought in mind? What attitude did you have toward that thought?

Chris tried a version of this experiment, walking around my office several times while holding this thought in mind. He recognized something familiar about this experience and also something different. He was quite familiar with walking around with what he called "stupid thoughts" in his mind, and this was one of them because his legs were clearly unbroken. What was different was his reaction to the "stupid thoughts." Never before had he walked around with a "stupid thought" in his mind and failed to get embroiled in arguing with it. This time, he simply walked around with the thought and didn't argue or get upset because he regarded it as one of my stupid thoughts, rather than his!

Chris could clearly see that he didn't actively or deliberately create the stupid thoughts he found so aggravating. His brain produced these unwanted thoughts the same way his stomach would sometimes produce unwanted noises. This experiment helped him see that he could simply carry in his head my "stupid thought" about his legs being broken as he walked around my office without taking it too seriously or arguing with it. It also raised the possibility that perhaps he could walk around with *his own* "stupid thoughts" and not get embroiled in arguing with them either. Perhaps you too, with practice, can find ways to walk around with the worrisome thoughts you find so exaggerated and unhelpful without becoming embroiled in arguing with them.

Take Your Worry with You

All too often, people get tricked into thinking that they have to get rid of intrusive worrisome thoughts *before* they can move on to another activity. For instance, a woman beset by worrisome thoughts might decide to skip going to a dinner party because she thinks she won't be able to enjoy the experience with all those worrisome thoughts in her mind. She decides to stay home alone, where she's most likely to continue to obsess about her worries, rather than go to an activity where she might find something else to be of more interest.

What would be the opposite of that? Take the worry thoughts with you as you go to another location or activity with an attitude of acceptance for the experience of having unwanted, unpleasant, worrisome thoughts. Creating a poem or song from your worry will help you cultivate that attitude of acceptance.

Reply with "Yes, and…"

This is the cardinal rule of improvisational theater: "Yes, and…" It means that whatever your scene partner says to you, find some way to agree with it and add another element to keep the scene moving. Should your scene partner say to you, "I'm so concerned; I don't know where the cat has gone!" it would be unhelpful to the scene to deny what he just said. For instance, an unhelpful reply in this scene might be "What? You don't have a cat!" A "Yes, and…" reply might be something like, "The cat food is missing also. I think he's been catnapped!"

You can use "Yes, and…" responses to your own what-if worrisome thoughts. Chris might respond to his frequent thought, *What if the boss gives me a poor evaluation?* by replying, *Yes, and he'll probably hit on my wife too and steal her from me once I've been fired!* It's a simple way to humor the thoughts without getting into an argument with yourself.

Here's the Cadillac of exercises for humoring the worry rather than getting into a struggle with it.

Make Appointments for Your Worry

Schedule two ten-minute appointments each day. Pick times when you can have privacy, without interruptions from anyone, including pets and children, and turn off your cell phone. If at all possible, pick a location that includes a mirror. Sometimes your parked car is a good choice. Years ago, clients used to be hesitant about doing this in their car and possibly being seen talking to themselves. Now, however, people will just assume you're talking on your phone!

When the appointed time arrives, worry aloud in front of a mirror. Fill the ten minutes with worry as best you can, and let it be pure, unadulterated worry: no research, no problem solving, no reassuring, just one what-if thought after another. You might find it helpful to set a timer.

This doesn't sound like fun, and it's not. The potential benefit is this. It's pretty clear that we can't simply tell our-selves, "Stop thinking or worrying about that," and make that work. If that worked, you wouldn't be reading this book because you'd be enjoying the worry-free life suggested by those friends and family who tell you, "Don't worry about it!" That doesn't work for most people.

But most people who make regular use of worry appoint-ments do find that they get pretty good, not at stopping their worry, but at postponing it. When they find themselves wor-rying outside of their scheduled worry appointments, they give themselves this choice: either do ten minutes of worry on this topic now or postpone it until the next scheduled worry appointment. This enables most people to sweep relatively clear large portions of their day that used to be continually interrupted by worry. It's not a perfect solution, but it's pretty good.

Thinking It Over

Chronic anxiety is a counterintuitive experience, and nothing is more counterintuitive than intrusive worrisome thoughts. People are often nervous about allowing and accepting these anxious thoughts. Some people even fear that they can make bad things happen just by thinking of them. However, the counterintuitive reply of humoring and playing with the thoughts, rather than resisting and arguing with them, is perhaps one of the best ways to respond to this kind of worry.

In the next chapter, we'll take a look at what happens when people try to use distraction and thought stopping to get relief from worrisome thoughts. And we'll look at an alternative method, a response that's the opposite of distraction and thought stopping.

Chapter 7

Observe, Don't Distract

You might now be wondering, *How about if I distract myself when I get anxious? How about if I make myself stop thinking about worrisome topics and think about something pleasant?*

The short answer is no. Trying to suppress or remove your anxious thoughts will generally make your situation worse rather than better. When it comes to anxiety symptoms, what you resist, persists.

So I'm going to suggest something really counterintuitive: I suggest you take notes during your anxious episodes, and I'll give you a pair of journals you can use for this purpose.

But first, here's the longer answer.

How Distraction Works—and Doesn't

When you get distracted from anxious thoughts and sensations by some event outside of you, it often relieves the anxiety. A person experiencing a panic attack who receives an unexpected phone call from a long-lost friend will often stop panicking as his attention turns to the surprise and joy of the conversation.

Deliberately trying to distract yourself from anxious thoughts and sensations, however, is not so helpful. There's a big difference between being spontaneously distracted by an event and trying deliberately to change the topic in your own mind. The first one works pretty well, as our brain naturally turns its attention to the unexpected event. That's what brains do; they turn our attention to new and unexpected events. The second one works poorly. When we instruct ourselves to stop thinking of something, we are also reminding ourselves of the topic we don't want to think about. That's more like arguing with yourself than distraction.

Clinical research on the topic says that when we try to get rid of a thought, it tends to recur. The traditional experiment with this is to take a minute or two and not think of a white bear.[6] Try that for a minute now, if you like. If you get the results most people do, you'll soon have an entire family of polar bears roaming around your mind.

However, the fact that you want to distract yourself from anxiety symptoms can be a useful reminder to you about the nature of the problem. What does it tell you about a problem if you're motivated to distract yourself from it?

My clients usually respond with answers like these:

It's dangerous.

Outsmart Your Anxious Brain

It's an overwhelming problem that I can't solve.

It's shameful or embarrassing.

Let's suppose you're standing in line in a bank, and a bank robbery starts, with gunshots. How likely are you to take out your checkbook and start balancing your account to distract yourself from the gunfire?

Not so likely, right? When we're motivated to distract ourselves from a problem, it tells us the chips aren't down right now. We're not facing any clear and present danger. That's what makes it okay to distract myself. If I see a runaway bus heading toward me, I'm not going to sing a happy song to distract myself. I'm going to run and jump to safety! When you feel the urge to distract yourself from something, that can be a powerful reminder that you're not in any clear and present danger. If you were, you'd be protecting, not distracting yourself.

If you could simply dismiss your what-if thoughts on realizing this, that would be fine. But all too often our efforts to dismiss and distract ourselves from thoughts yield the opposite result. How can we even tell if we're succeeding at distraction? We have to examine our thoughts to see if they contain the forbidden one—and now we're thinking about it again!

Thought Stopping and Other Problems

The traditional thought-stopping technique has you snapping a rubber band against your wrist and telling yourself, "Stop!" when you experience unwanted thoughts. That's pretty much the idea: hurt yourself and tell yourself to stop thinking about that subject you just thought of. It's contrary to all the research on thought suppression, which tells us that the main effect of thought suppression is thought rebound, and that suppression of a thought inevitably leads to its return.[7] When clients ask me if thought stopping is a good idea, I always say the same thing. "Thought stopping? Don't even think about thought stopping!"

Deliberate thought stopping works pretty much like banning books—it draws your attention back to the forbidden material. It also suggests, much like book bans do, that thoughts can be dangerous. Thoughts aren't dangerous. You can have thoughts of dangerous actions, but only actions can be dangerous.

Maybe you've had some sessions of cognitive behavioral therapy (CBT), or read some self-help books based on CBT methods. If you have, you've probably been introduced to cognitive restructuring. This is a method in which you notice some of the errors in your fearful thinking, correct them, and then go on about your business with less anxiety because you've corrected the "errors in your thinking."

I've used CBT methods throughout my career as a psychologist. What I find most helpful in CBT is the *B* part, helping people to change their *behavior*—what they do. That's been very effective in helping people overcome chronic anxiety disorders. I find that cognitive restructuring is often less helpful to clients struggling with chronic anxiety disorders, particularly when they're struggling with lots of worrisome thoughts.

I think that's because this kind of worry doesn't follow any of our rules of logic and evidence. It's not based on what's likely, or even possible. It's based on what would be scary and terrible. Trying to identify and correct the errors in this kind of thinking is like arguing with a person who offers no logic or evidence, only opinion. It just leads to more arguing.

My view about the use of cognitive restructuring with chronic what-if worry is that it's too similar to thought stopping to be helpful. It's often unhelpful with chronic what-if worry because there isn't an actual problem to be solved, only worry to be contended with. Many of my clients have expressed frustration, and even concerns that they are deficient somehow, because they don't get much benefit from cognitive restructuring. What's more likely to be true is that they don't get much benefit from cognitive restructuring because it's not so well suited for chronic worry.

Distraction, cognitive restructuring, and thought stopping involve resisting and controlling your thoughts. The opposite would be simply observing your thoughts and writing them down. You might think that you've already done too much observing of these thoughts, that what you want is to stop having them entirely. That might be nice if it were available without all the negative side effects that come from resisting. But if your experience with opposing these thoughts suggests that it rarely, if ever, gives you a good result, maybe it's time to try something very different. Observing can be the counterintuitive response to worry that helps you let it go, rather than build it up.

Anxiety Journals

One of the best ways of being an observer is to take some written notes about your experience while it's happening, the same way a reporter would. I'm not talking about free-form journaling. Rather, I suggest you complete a questionnaire about your anxiety while you are experiencing it. I have two. The Panic Journal is for panic attacks and phobic responses that include a lot of physical symptoms. The Worry Journal is for anxiety episodes that are composed mostly of worrisome what-if thoughts. They're available online at http://www.newharbinger.com/41993.

I suggest you fill out these forms *while* you're having a panic attack, a phobic experience, or obsessive what-if thoughts.

Outsmart Your Anxious Brain

If this idea sounds unwelcome at first, you have plenty of company! My clients don't usually like the idea much at first. They don't want to stay at the scene of a panic attack or a phobic situation; they don't want to be having these thoughts, much less writing them down; they doubt they'll subsequently be able to read what they wrote; and they worry they'll feel self-conscious about taking notes in a grocery store or a church.

And yet...what would you guess is the usual reaction of a person having a panic attack when they actually start filling out the Panic Journal? It's pretty much the opposite of what they expected! The panic starts to subside as they fill out the questionnaire. It usually declines rather than increases. And it's frequently the same with the Worry Journal as well.

When I ask clients to explain this unexpected result, they often say that the journal *distracted* them. But here, too, they are getting tricked. What kind of distraction is it that keeps mentioning the name, be it panic or worry, of the thing you fear? What kind of distraction asks you for more details about the thing you fear? The journals are very helpful for several reasons, but not because they distract you.

Take a look at the journal that seems most relevant to you—the Panic Journal if you have lots of physical symptoms that scare you or the Worry Journal if your symptoms are mostly what-if thoughts.

The Worry Journal will direct your attention in these ways:

- It reminds you that the worry will end, at a time when you might have forgotten that, by asking you to time it.

- It asks you to rate the intensity of your present worry.

- It guides you to diagram the worry sentence, which will help you notice the worry invitation of "What if?"

- It guides you to apply the Two-Part Test to your worry.

- It asks you to identify what triggered the present worry.

- It helps you break down the anxiety into the different symptoms you're experiencing.

- It reminds you to notice, and perhaps modify, your breathing and what you're doing with the muscles of your upper body.

- It helps you identify and evaluate the fearful predictions contained within your worry.

- It helps you assess your choices of potential actions and reminds you of the types of responses that are most likely to be helpful in the moment.

The Panic Journal will direct your attention in this manner:

- It reminds you that the panic will end, by asking you to time it.

- It asks you to rate the strength of the panic episode.

- It asks you to list your symptoms by category.

- It asks you to note the type of panic by noticing any situational aspects.

- It asks what you were doing and thinking before the panic.

- It asks what you fear the panic will do to you.

- It asks about your breathing.

- It asks what you are doing to soothe yourself.

- It asks if you're using any safety behaviors.

- It asks how the attack ends.

- It asks about your feared outcome.

- It asks your thoughts about the next time.

Find a way to incorporate these journals into your daily routine. One of the two is probably more relevant to you than the other, so focus on that one. Keep a small supply in your purse, briefcase, glove box, backpack, or wherever else might be handy should you experience an anxiety episode. If you habitually carry a bottle of Xanax with you, fold a journal up really small and put it in the bottle! That can help remind you to consider using the journal before taking the Xanax. If you prefer to work digitally, store the journal on your digital device and work with it there.

Observe in the Moment

Complete the journals *during* the anxiety episode. Some of the journal items will remind you of helpful responses you can have in a moment of high anxiety, and if you wait until later to use the journal, you won't benefit from the reminders. You'll also get a more complete picture when you write the journal entry at the height of an anxiety episode rather than later.

Clients often remark, as we review their journals, that they don't remember writing down some of the observations they made! High anxiety often disrupts memory in ways that make recounting the experience difficult. When you fill out the journal right on the spot, it gives you a better chance to notice some of the subtle tricks anxiety plays to get you so afraid and makes it easier for you to navigate a similar experience in the future.

Store your journals for subsequent review. It will be helpful to review them from time to time to look for trends and changes in how you are responding.

You will probably face some circumstances where it seems undesirable, or even dangerous, to complete a journal form. People are sometimes hesitant to fill them out in public places, like grocery stores, churches, and restaurants, for fear of calling attention to themselves. Generally this is more the result of feeling self-conscious than the prospect of any actual inquiry from strangers. You'll never really know if anyone wondered what you were writing, but very few strangers will be so bold as to ask! If someone does, just say you're writing notes to yourself. Use a clipboard to make it look even more ordinary and easier to write.

Writing in a journal while you're driving a car, on the other hand, is a bad idea! But it will be good to observe the fears you experience while driving. You could perhaps use a voice-activated recorder or a recording app on your (hands-free) cell phone to record your answers. If you have a trusted support person with you, have them ask you the questions and record your answers while you drive.

Regular use of the journals is also likely to foster a notable shift in your attitude toward the anxiety experience. When you use the journals as I've suggested, it helps you take on the role of observer—someone who takes a more accepting and passive role toward the symptoms you're noting and recording.

Observer Versus Victim Postures

There are two basic postures from which you can respond to worry, panic, and anxiety. One is the victim posture, in which you respond instinctively as one who is being threatened and in need of immediate protection. This is the posture in which people are motivated to distract themselves from anxious thoughts and symptoms, responses that tend to make the worries more persistent.

The other is the observer posture, in which you take careful note of all the symptoms and circumstances coming to your attention without resistance, protection, distraction, or even any strong judgments. You're observing your thoughts, as best you can, without evaluating or reacting to their content. This is what Claire Weekes meant by "floating": observing your thoughts and letting time pass without reacting.

The more you are in the victim role, the less available you are to observe anything because you are struggling with your own thoughts. This is why people have so much trouble describing their first panic attack. So terrorized and victimized did they feel that they were unable to observe the events in a way they could later remember and describe. The reverse is also true. The more you are in the observer role, the less available you are to feel victimized and struggle with your symptoms. This is what makes the role of observer so useful.

Using a Symptom Inventory

Here's another way to use the observer role when you're practicing with a feared object or situation. It's particularly useful for phobias in which you're cast in a passive role, like a passenger in a vehicle or a patient in a waiting room.

Create a list of all the symptoms you expect to experience when you encounter your phobic object or situation, be it dogs, heights, crowds, or whatever. Have a separate list for each of the four types of anxiety symptoms:

- Physical sensations

- Fearful thoughts

- Strong negative emotions

- Frightened behaviors

Give this enough time and thought that you can develop a good, comprehensive inventory of virtually every symptom you might experience in your feared situation. Cast a broad net, including the less likely ones along with the sure bets. Once you have a thorough inventory of all the symptoms you might experience, write your list on the Symptom Inventory (which you can find online at http://www.newharbinger.com /41993), and bring it with you when you do exposure practice. During your exposure time, keep a simple count of how often you experience each symptom by putting a mark in a box each time one occurs.

What makes this effective? You're simply observing and counting the symptoms rather than trying to distract yourself from them. The simple act of counting is a great way to help you more fully occupy the role of observer.

Thinking It Over

Far from being a useful tool, distraction in all its varieties serves to maintain and enhance anxiety troubles, rather than relieve them. Finding ways to more fully occupy the role of observer will help you acquire an awareness of your symptoms coupled with a more detached attitude toward them. The anxiety journals and the Symptom Inventory are good ways to occupy the role of observer.

In the next chapter, we'll take a look at the effects of relying on "support people" and consider alternatives.

Chapter 8

Let Your Support People Go!

People who struggle with anxiety disorders often rely on "support people" (also called "safe people") to help them cope with the situations, activities, and objects they fear. In the presence of support people, they often do more of life's activities—travel, shop in crowded stores, interact with people—than they believe they can manage on their own. Unfortunately, this opportunity to engage in life activities comes with a high price. It tricks you into believing that you can't and couldn't handle these situations on your own and leads you to feel more dependent and less capable over time.

The opposite of relying on a support person is doing things alone. That's a scary idea for people who have come to rely heavily on the presence of a support person. For now, be aware that you don't have to go it alone all at once, without any planning. You can take steps at a pace that works for you. But letting your support people go is the way to counter the trick of feeling so dependent on others and regain your ability to rely on yourself.

How This Trick Works: The Fear of Large Stores

Cynthia fears shopping in large, crowded stores. *What if I panic while I'm there?* she worries. She's never found a satisfactory answer to this question. She fears that terrible things will happen to her while she struggles to maintain her composure in a slow-moving line or the rear of a store with a confusing layout and no obvious path to an exit. She realizes that her fears are exaggerated and unrealistic, but that doesn't reduce her fear when she starts to panic. The solution that naturally occurred to her soon after her first panic attack was to always make sure she has company while shopping in such places. And, as is so often the case with problems of anxiety, she found a solution that was actually another problem. She got tricked into relying on the presence and reassurance of others in ways that made her anxiety worse rather than better. She didn't become a calmer, more capable person; she became a more dependent one.

Today Cynthia relies principally on her husband Hal to serve as her support person when she goes grocery shopping. Cynthia was originally satisfied as long as he was in the store, but as time went on, she found it more and more necessary that he be right at her side. When he does wander off, she keeps her cell phone handy, ready to text him immediately should she start to panic.

On "good" days Cynthia sometimes agrees to let Hal wait in the car, as long as she can call him if she needs "help." She used to occasionally drive to a store on her own as long as she could chat with him on her cell phone while entering the store. But on one such occasion, Hal's phone ran out of power. Cynthia hasn't driven to a store on her own since that happened.

Hal doesn't do anything to keep Cynthia safe because she's not in any danger. She's just very afraid of having a panic attack. He just hangs out with her as they shop. When she feels anxious, she tells him she's afraid and needs to leave. He usually encourages her to stay and finish the shopping, but if she continues to get more anxious, he'll agree that they should leave, and he accompanies her to the cashier. Sometimes she feels so frightened that he pays for their purchases while she paces outside the store.

Is this a good thing or a bad thing? It depends on how you define the problem. If the problem is simply getting the shopping done, then you might think this is a good thing because Hal's presence makes it easier for Cynthia to shop. The shopping gets done. Of course, it could also get done by having Hal do the shopping or by using a delivery service. Cynthia doesn't particularly want to use those solutions because she feels bad about herself when she feels unable to do the shopping, and she'd like to get over these fears.

The real problem isn't getting the shopping done; it's getting over these fears. Does Hal's role as a support person help or hurt the goal of getting over these fears? It hurts! The shopping gets done when Hal accompanies her, but Cynthia's fear of the stores is strengthened and maintained by her reliance on Hal's presence. Each and every time she shops in the company of her support person, she's reinforced in her belief that she couldn't have done it without him and that terrible things would have happened had she attempted it on her own. These beliefs lead her to become more fearful and dependent over time, rather than less. *What if something happens, and he's not available?* she worries. She's even been troubled by the thought, *What if Hal dies before I do?*

Eleanor, whom we met in chapter 1, had a terrible fear that she would faint if she drove at night. However, she was able to hold down a night job three nights each week and hadn't fainted, not once, in more than ten years of driving to this job. Each time she drove to work, her husband trailed her in his car, and she attributed her safety to his presence. As long as she could see him in the rearview mirror, she felt reassured that all would be well, and she was able to keep her job. But what a terrible price to pay, continuing to believe that she was subject to fainting at any time should he get a flat or have some mechanical breakdown.

Here are some common methods support people use in an effort to be helpful:

- Staying next to you, or at very close range, at all times during the task

- Promising you that all will be well and that you won't become afraid

- Distracting you from anxiety with chatter and conversation

- Intervening on your behalf with store clerks or other people on the scene

- Making decisions on your behalf

- Offering ongoing support—rubbing your back, offering you water, reminding you that you can leave at any time, and so forth—even when you haven't asked for it

- Doing the driving or driving in the areas where you feel most vulnerable

If you rely on support people, it probably enables you to engage in some activities you would otherwise avoid and perhaps even to feel a lower level of anxiety as you do. But does it help you to regain your confidence that you can engage in these activities on your own? That's what's most important.

Take a little time to consider your experience with support people carefully. Write a brief description of your experience with support people in your notebook. Include the following information in your description:

- Who is your primary support person? Is there more than one?

- Identify the activities, locations, objects, and so on that your support person helps you cope with.

- Describe what your support person does, if anything, to calm you.

- Describe how your fear, anxiety, and worry have evolved during the time you've relied on support people.

- How has your reliance on support people affected your sense of being free, confident, and independent?

- Has your reliance on this support person affected the quality of your relationship?

- If so, has it had a positive or a negative effect?

- Has your reliance on support people given you some benefits, in terms of comfort and convenience that you enjoy?

- Are you willing to make that trade, to give up that extra measure of comfort and convenience, in order to foster your recovery?

If your review suggests that there are long-term drawbacks to your reliance on support people, then you will probably benefit from phasing out your reliance on them. Sounds scary, I know. But this is what will help you discover that you can manage on your own and regain your sense of competence and independence. This is the direction I take with my phobic clients who want to regain their freedom to come and go as they please without being hobbled by their fears.

You don't need to let them go all at once. How fast you move with your recovery work matters much less than going in the right direction. As long as you're moving in the right direction—in this case, in the direction of being independent and confident in your ability to handle everyday tasks—you can expect to attain the recovery you seek.

It's essential that the person with the fear take the lead in reviewing and making changes in their reliance on a support person. It's not helpful for the support person to try to force changes or spring any surprises. If you're a support person reading this and want to do something positive for your friend, initiate a conversation about this and invite your friend to read this book, but don't take charge. The person with the fear has to be in charge of this.

Some people will do it all at once, essentially "firing" their support person and going out into their feared situations without that assistance. That's okay if you feel willing and able to do that. Others find it easier to in a series of small steps. You can judge for yourself how fast or slow to go. Try a small step or two, see how that works for you, and then decide if you want to pick up the pace or not.

Here are some ways you can break this process—of letting go of your reliance on support people—into smaller steps:

- Have a conversation with your support person. Identify the way the two of you work together and the rules of thumb the two of you use, and gradually reduce the number of specific ways the support person helps you.

- Reduce the time the support person spends with you. If they accompany you in the store, perhaps you can have them arrive a few minutes after you enter the store, leave the store a few minutes before you, or step out of the store for a few minutes in the middle of shopping. Gradually increase these intervals over time.

- Reduce the spoken and physical interaction between the two of you. If you're used to having your support person right next to you as you

Outsmart Your Anxious Brain

walk down an aisle, perhaps one of you can change directions. Enter an aisle from opposite ends, walking in opposite directions so you only pass each other in the middle. Do the same in the next aisle.

- Systematically, one step at a time, begin to leave your support person out of your daily activities. Identify all the various situations and activities in which your support person accompanies you, and rank them in terms of which seem the most anxiety provoking to you. Then you can begin to leave your support person behind as you tackle the least anxiety-provoking activity and move up the list over time.

- If you can see that the role of your support person has grown over time, shrink it by reversing that process. First review the history of how your support person has assisted you over the years. It might have started accidentally, when you realized it was a source of comfort for this person to be with you. Maybe initially it included just one or two triggers and came to expand over time. Maybe it became more deliberate and intentional over time. You can trace the way this behavior developed and grew; then reverse the process. Begin shrinking it down in the opposite way it expanded and grew.

- Increase the distance between you, first within the store or other location, gradually keeping the person at a farther and farther distance. Gradually replace the person's physical presence with phone contact and diminish that as well. A final step here might be to periodically leave your cell phone home entirely. We'll check that out in the next chapter.

You don't need to do this all at once. You can always find ways to break the task into smaller steps. For instance, if your support person is used to providing lots of verbal reassurance, find ways to reduce the amount. You might put a time limit on it—waiting at least five minutes, for instance, after requesting verbal reassurance before doing it again. You might ask your support person not to initiate verbal reassurance at all. Instead, make an agreement that if you want some verbal reassurance, you will specifically ask for it. If there are some standard phrases or ideas that your support person tells you time and time again, have that person write them down on some three-by-five cards and flash the card at you rather than repeat the reassurance out loud. One final step in phasing out your support person might be to tell them to stay home and to carry their photo instead!

What might get in your way as you start to reduce your reliance on your support person? Probably the main obstacle people experience is that they will initially feel less comfortable and more frightened as they reduce their dependence on the support person. People often hear this question in their mind as they consider doing this: *Why am I doing this? I'm feeling more afraid!*

That temporary increase in fear is *precisely* the reason to do this. If you've become dependent on a support person, or any other anti-anxiety technique, you feel protected, temporarily, from the fear, rather than genuinely safe. That sets the stage for you to have more anxiety going forward as you wonder if your protection will always be available.

Keep in mind that you are only reducing the amount of comfort you obtain from the presence of your support person as you take these steps. You're not increasing any danger because an anxiety disorder isn't dangerous to begin with. That's what makes exposure a useful tactic for anxiety disorders. We don't do exposure to tigers!

What should you do about the discomfort you experience while making this planned reduction in your reliance on a support person? Be clear with yourself that you will feel increased anxiety at first and plan on accepting and working with it. Be wary of "hoping" that you won't feel anxious! For most people, "hoping" that they won't feel anxious is just another label for worrying.

And use the AWARE steps (chapter 4) as a guide:

Accept.

Watch

Act

Repeat

End

Eleanor first sought help with her fear of fainting while driving at night because of the disruptive effect it was having on her marriage. Her life with her husband was increasingly focused on the need for him to follow her wherever she drove at night. Neither of them liked how it was affecting their relationship, and both wanted to find a solution.

It seemed plain to me that if Eleanor got some practice driving at night without her husband following her, she would come to see that she would feel anxious temporarily, but she wouldn't faint. But this was too large a step for her to take. If she had been able to simply tell her husband to stay home and drive everywhere herself, she wouldn't have needed to seek out any help at all! Instead, she agreed to start having her husband gradually increase the distance between their cars by just a little bit to see how that affected things. Sure enough, it sometimes made her more nervous, but she never fainted. Once she had some successes with allowing her husband to follow at a greater distance, we agreed to treat the therapy as a research project. The purpose of this research project was to determine the maximum range over which her husband could project this anti-fainting power. And, surprisingly, we found he could do it from the comfort and convenience of their home!

In this same way, you can begin to phase out your reliance on the presence and reassurance of others until you arrive at the point where you are content to handle your activities alone.

Your relationship with this person is likely to change as you become more independent. It will be helpful for you to consider how you want the relationship to change and what you value about it. A married couple often finds that their relationship has suffered and narrowed as one spouse has become more and more involved in the role of support person. It will be helpful for such couples to talk about the changes and find ways to restore the fun and companionship that used to be part of their marriage before the anxiety became so prominent. This will be true of other relationships and friendships as well. Just because you decide to "fire" your support person doesn't mean they can't be part of your life. In fact, it will probably enrich your life if the two of you can shift your relationship back to being two independent people who enjoy each other's company rather than needing it for reassurance.

Thinking It Over

Most people obtain a short-term benefit from reliance on support people, but at the cost of maintaining and strengthening their anxiety over time. You will probably benefit from a careful review of the way reliance on support people has crept into your life and how it functions now. Consider both the benefits you get from it, probably in comfort and convenience, and the price you pay, probably reduced freedom and greater phobic avoidance. Then, if you see a benefit to reducing your reliance on support people, you can begin to do that a step at a time, at a pace that suits you.

In the next chapter, we'll examine a closely related trick, the reliance on support objects.

Chapter 9

Leave Support Objects at Home

Support objects are items that people take with them in an effort to minimize the anxiety they feel when they venture outside of their "safe zone." Support objects function in much the same way as support people, except that you won't get any backtalk from support objects. Common support objects include medications, comfort animals, water bottles, cell phones, pictures of the grandkids, snack foods, items thought to possess "good luck," books, and more.

Reliance on a support object typically provides a short-term benefit and a long-term disadvantage. People often feel less anxious and get more of their daily activities done when they bring support objects with them. That's the short-term benefit. However, people often feel "protected" by the object in ways that suggest they couldn't function well on their own without it. That's the long-term disadvantage. Reliance on the support object usually decreases your sense of being able to manage life's challenges on your own. It maintains and strengthens your anxiety long term, rather than reduces it.

The long-term disadvantage most people experience usually far outweighs the value of the temporary reduction in anxiety they get from relying on a support object. But people often get fooled because they get the short-term reduction in anxiety *immediately*. You will be better off, when tempted by the prospect of an immediate, but temporary, reduction in anxiety, to select the option that has no long-term disadvantages. That usually means letting go of support objects.

Some support objects could be useful in an emergency but are principally used to resist and divert anxiety. Cell phones, for instance, could be used to call 911 for emergency help, but I've never had a client actually need to do that. The phones are typically used for distracting conversation and to seek reassurance. People who worry about their ability to swallow or have fears of dehydration find comfort in knowing that they have a bottle of water with them, but typically don't need to drink the water to stay safe. The water bottle simply reassures them that they'll be okay. Other objects, such as lucky shirts and pictures of the grandkids, are more obviously without any function other than being a source of emotional comfort and reassurance.

At first glance, support objects don't seem to be much of a problem. If you can feel less anxious and get more of your daily tasks done by carrying a water bottle or a favorite self-help book, what's the harm in that? Maybe you've been encouraged in your use of support objects by friends and family, or even mental health professionals, who suggested or endorsed your use of them.

However, the truth is that support objects trick you and are part of the problem rather than the solution.

Support Objects Undermine Your Self-Reliance

Support objects trick you by suggesting that you managed to handle a feared situation or activity only with the help of that object. Your belief that the object enabled you to stay—in a crowded grocery store or theater despite your fear of a panic attack, or in the doctor's waiting room despite your fearful thoughts of having a dreaded disease—prevents you from taking full credit for what you did because you give some of the credit to the object rather than yourself. Reliance on support objects can lead you to believe that the object "saved" you in some way and undermine your confidence in yourself over time. It also creates the additional worry, *What if I lose, or forget, or break my object? Then I'll be in big trouble!*

Reliance on support objects also leads people to go to great lengths to ensure that they have the object with them. If you believed that all that stood between you and over-whelming panic was a water bottle, would one bottle be enough? Maybe it occurs to you to keep a case in the trunk of your car! In this way, people become more and more dependent on their supply of support objects, feel more anxious and concerned about their availability, and feel less powerful and more vulnerable within themselves.

Notes on Support Objects

Medications. Some people use medications (usually the benzodiazepines, like Xanax and Klonopin) much more like a support object than a prescription drug. They take them with them everywhere they go, but don't usually swallow them. They feel comforted and reassured simply by touching the bottle in their pocket or pocketbook. That's how good these medications are—you get relief just by touching the bottle!

If you've ever reached for your Xanax or Klonopin and felt better even before the pill passed your lips, you're getting the same placebo effect. You feel better just knowing you have the pill, even before it's entered your system and started working.

Cell phones. People with a variety of anxiety disorders often come to regard their cell phone as a basic necessity. They're no more likely to leave the house without their cell phone than they are to leave without clothes. They use it in an attempt to prevent anxiety in a variety of ways, including having reassuring contact with support people; distracting themselves with photos, conversations, music, and podcasts; and using their GPS to avoid any unexpected traffic. There's nothing wrong with these functions unless you think they protected or saved you somehow. If you do, you'll come to feel more dependent on that phone and less secure in your own abilities to handle life. That means more, not less, anxiety going forward.

You might find it unwelcome and unnatural to leave home without your cell phone. You'd need a real good reason to do that. Maybe overcoming your worry and fears is that good reason. You don't need to stop using a cell phone, but if you rely on your cell phone for assistance and reassurance with anxiety, you may find a benefit from doing some exposure practice without it handy.

Luck. Items without even that much of a connection to your realistic needs include "lucky" objects—articles of clothing, a rabbit's foot or a lucky coin, almost anything that can be pressed into service as a lucky item. This is basically a superstitious behavior. I've met many clients over the years who remembered the particular clothes they wore when they had a first panic attack and made sure they never wore that outfit again.

Most people can see that these safety items can't really protect them but justify them with the idea, "It can't hurt!" But it does hurt. It hurts by persuading you that you might have been protected by a lucky sweater or some other object. This idea strengthens the belief that you're not strong, independent, brave, or smart enough to cope on your own. It also persuades you that you are actually in danger when you're much more likely facing discomfort.

Comfort animals. A comfort or emotional support animal is an animal that has received no particular training to do anything for you when you need help but is the source of companionship and emotional comfort. By comparison, a service animal has received specific training to do something for its owner when the owner is in need of assistance.

Having a pet at home can be a wonderful source of companionship and pleasure, and a source of anxiety reduction as well. But a problem arises when people feel dependent on their animal in order to travel outside their home—to board an airplane, attend a class, or visit a restaurant. Over time, as they rely on the presence of the animal to convince themselves that they can cope with the external world, they are likely to feel more vulnerable and less independent, less able to venture out on their own without feeling anxious. A person who boards an airplane or train with a comfort animal still does everything that a passenger needs to do. But they don't take all the credit for it! Instead, they attribute their ability to be okay as a passenger to the animal rather than themselves. They get tricked by the presence of their comfort animal, and this is the biggest negative about traveling with one.

The opposite of traveling with these animals is traveling without them, and this will probably be a valuable part of exposure practice for most people.

It might seem to you as though it's a bad idea to leave your support objects at home. You might anticipate, probably correctly, that you'll have some anxious thoughts about the "bad luck" that might come your way if you leave them at home, and you might worry that such anxious thoughts are a big problem. "Wouldn't it be just my luck," clients have said to me, "that the day I go out without my [cell phone, water bottle, Xanax, family pictures] turns out to be the day that I needed it most?'" "Wouldn't it be ironic," my groups of fearful flyers often say, "if we crashed while there was a group of fearful flyers on board?"

Such thoughts often scare my clients. What's actually happening here? When you try to prevent the appearance of these anxious thoughts by carrying objects with you, it's like you're being blackmailed. And unfortunately, when you pay off the blackmailers, it probably just means that they'll be back again in the near future, demanding new payoffs. It's the same with anxious thoughts. You make yourself feel more vulnerable by carrying objects to protect yourself from anxiety and worry. You don't get off the hook by paying blackmail, and you don't get off the hook by defending against anxiety with objects.

You'll probably feel more anxious at first, doing exposure without your object. That's okay; that's the whole point of exposure—to practice feeling anxious. Practicing experiencing the fears, rather than avoiding or preventing them, is what will help you see that you can handle these scary thoughts, emotions, sensations, and behaviors without the water bottle, lucky sweater, or any other object.

Getting Started

A good way to start reducing your dependence on support objects is by making a written inventory of all your support objects in your notebook. List each object and the benefit you suppose it provides. Here are some items from some of my clients' inventories.

Object	Immediate Benefit
Cell phone	Distraction calls, emergency help, distraction with games and photos
Water bottle	Reassurance that throat works, counters fears of dehydration
Pictures of loved ones	Make me smile and feel less anxious
Xanax	Protects me from panic
Lucky shirt	Protects me from crashing, having a heart attack, or "freaking out" and being subdued by the other passengers

Comfort animal	Distracts me from having a panic attack or other episode of high anxiety

Make an initial draft in your notebook; then come back to it a few times during the next few days because you'll probably think of more. Some support objects are subtle habits, and you might not recognize all of them at first.

Once you have a fairly complete list of your support objects, consider how your reliance on each one affects both your immediate comfort and your long-term freedom. For instance, some people obtain immediate comfort by always having a water bottle handy. It reduces their worries about having trouble swallowing something (maybe their Xanax!), about dehydration, dry mouth, and other things. And a cool drink of water feels good on a hot day. They get some immediate and temporary comfort.

But they also pay a price, the price that comes with attributing their safety to the presence of a water bottle. If my life and sanity depend on the presence of a bottle of water, how secure can I feel? It can always spill or run out. The more I rely on that bottle, the more vulnerable I'm likely to feel, and the more likely I am to limit my travel around town and other activities as well.

Lessons Learned from Exposure

You can probably guess that my clients typically don't die, go crazy, faint, burn down the neighborhood, cause terrible car crashes, or experience any of the many catastrophes they fear as they do their exposure practice. They're encouraged by that, but it's not enough to bring them the recovery they seek.

They also need a good explanation of why they *didn't* experience the feared catastrophe when they flew on a plane, drove on a highway, stopped resisting their negative thoughts, used the stove at breakfast, and many other exposures. One of the questions I find myself asking my clients again and again, as they practice exposure work, is this: *To what do you attribute your failure to experience the catastrophe you feared?*

If you practice with the objects, situations, and activities you fear but bring support objects to the exposure task, you're very likely to attribute your success to the presence of the objects (or the support person, for that matter). As long as you feel protected and calmed by the objects, you'll continue to feel vulnerable and at risk in the future. That's why it's usually so important for adults to let go of the support objects.

Quick note to parents. If you're reading this book because you want to help your child with an anxiety disorder, be aware that it's different with children. Young children naturally rely on security blankets, parents, and other people and objects, as part of their natural development. They have more time and opportunity to outgrow their natural reliance on support objects, and so you can be much more permissive and gradual with a child who uses transitional objects. Adults, on the other hand, will probably need to let go of their support objects as part of their anxiety recovery work.

Letting go of your support objects would be an easy step to take if you were clearly getting no benefit from them. But you almost certainly are getting a benefit from them, and that's how you can get tricked.

If you manage to tiptoe through a short visit to the grocery store without having a panic attack because you have your cell phone ready to use, you got the benefit of not having a panic attack that time. But you got a very short-term, temporary benefit at the price of taking on a long-term disadvantage that will limit you long after the immediate and temporary comfort is gone.

The long-term disadvantage is that you feel "protected" by the cell phone in ways that lead you to feel more insecure and anxious in the future. You got a little relief from panic in the moments you spent in the store, but now you're much more prone to anticipatory anxiety about future visits to the store, more focused on your need for protection, and even more convinced that you can't manage on your own. It's like what happens when you borrow from a loan shark. You get the immediate cash you want today, but you pay and pay, at outrageously high rates of interest, throughout the future, and maybe get unpleasant visits from thugs.

This may very well be how your anxiety problem has grown over time. It's often a series of small steps in which you continued to take the short-term benefit of immediate relief and comfort while incurring a long-term problem of feeling weak and insecure. Often people don't even recognize how they're making this unfortunate trade, trading away their long-term freedom and independence for a few moments of brief, temporary comfort, until the phobia has really limited their freedom.

Each time you face a decision about your support object—whether to bring it with you this time or leave it at home—you're making a choice, often without recognizing it, between immediate short-term comfort and long-term progress and independence. It's similar to the choice we might have to make when we're trying to lose a little weight and hear a chocolate cookie calling to us from the kitchen. The cookie tastes great as soon as it enters my mouth, but there's a long-term price to pay for strengthening my habit of eating sweets.

It's so tempting to decide "I'll just have a little bite!"

Here's a decision rule that might help you firm up your determination to overcome anxiety when you have to make a specific choice of whether or not to rely on a support object.

It's this: only make choices that have no long-term disadvantages in your work to overcome chronic anxiety. Take the disadvantage now, in the form of present discomfort, rather than later in the form of loss of freedom. If you will apply this to the choices you face when you're tempted to wear that lucky sweater, bring Fido to the airport, or carry that water bottle while shopping, I think you'll find that it really helps foster your recovery.

Thinking It Over

Support objects tempt you with the prospect of an immediate moment of comfort and relief from anxiety and worry. However, a look at the fine print of this offer reveals that it comes with some long-term costs and disadvantages, which will hang around long after that brief moment of comfort has been forgotten. Check out the fine print! Aim to make the choice that doesn't have the long-term disadvantage of maintaining your anxiety and worry.

In the next chapter we'll look at how secrecy and shame conspire to maintain and strengthen worry and anxiety.

Chapter 10

The Truth Will Set You Free!

Secrecy and shame work hand in hand to strengthen and maintain anxiety and worry troubles. The more people feel ashamed of their troubles, the more likely they are to get tricked into hiding them and keeping them secret from others. The reverse is also true. The more people keep their troubles a secret, the more ashamed they will feel. It's a double whammy! Each one increases the other.

The opposite of secrecy is honesty, what psychologists often call self-disclosure. People who struggle with chronic anxiety and worry often feel so ashamed that the idea of self-disclosure is a nonstarter for them, and it might seem that way to you as well. But read this chapter before you decide whether or not disclosing your anxiety and worry might be useful to you. This is a self-help book, and you will choose what you use and what you discard. Feel free to check it out without any prior commitment!

Avoidance Is the Bait

Many people get tricked into trying to keep their anxiety problems a secret. They hope that if they hide their troubles from others, they will suffer less embarrassment. That's probably true, for a very short period of time. If you would feel embarrassed revealing your trouble to another person, you get the quick benefit of avoiding that embarrassment by keeping your anxiety a secret. That's the main effect of secrecy—sparing you immediate embarrassment. It's because so many anxiety sufferers keep their troubles a secret that we have millions and millions of people who think they're literally the only one to have these problems.

You probably know that there are intended effects (the good result you hope to get) and side effects (unpleasant additional problems you don't want) to medications. It's the same with secrecy. People often keep their anxiety and worry troubles a secret because they get the main effect of avoiding immediate embarrassment, and they like that. But there are lots of negative side effects to keeping your troubles a secret, and these are not so good. If you don't notice them, you can more easily be tricked into believing secrecy helps you, when it may actually cause you much more trouble than it's worth.

Let's consider some of the negative side effects of secrecy.

Imagining the Worst

Across all the anxiety disorders, people's anticipation of what will happen to them when they have an anxiety episode is almost always far worse than what they actually experience. People with panic attacks fear death and terrible loss of control, but when the panic attack actually arises, they typically become afraid and then calm down, with neither death nor loss of control. People with social anxiety fear terrible humiliation and ridicule from others, but when the social anxiety occurs, they feel embarrassed, and then life moves on. People with obsessive-compulsive disorder might feel certain that the neighborhood will burn because they didn't scrutinize the stove sufficiently, but when they get home from work, rarely do they see any fire trucks.

In a very similar way, your anticipation about how people would respond if they became aware of your anxiety and worry problems is probably far worse than what would actually occur. You may be attributing to your friends and family really negative and critical reactions, when in fact they may be far more sympathetic and accepting than you suspect. In fact, they may well experience some of the same troubles as you! When you keep your fears a secret from loved ones and friends, who are generally in your corner and have your interests at heart, you probably feel more criticized and rejected than would actually be the case if you revealed your difficulties. Instead of getting the support you might want, you suffer silently in your own self-criticism. You may think you know what family and friends would say if you shared your secret, but those are still your thoughts, not theirs.

Sometimes, not often, it does happen that a person gets a negative response to their self-disclosure. Even in those cases, life goes on. You can't expect to please everyone in life, and it's not necessary to try.

Feeling Like a Fraud

I've met some very talented, creative, and intelligent people who suffered with chronic anxiety and worry. They had many accomplishments in their lives, successes that would make anyone proud. But all too often, they dismissed their accomplishments. They couldn't take any pride in them because they believed "if people knew my ugly secret of anxiety and worry, they wouldn't be so impressed by me." They thought they were frauds. The main reason they continued to see themselves as frauds was because they kept their troubles a secret. They remained in their mind, wrestling with their own shame and blame, rather than bringing it out into the open where it could more readily be accepted and dismissed.

Increased Worry

When you try to keep information hidden with lies and excuses, it can be challenging to keep your story straight. If you've given different excuses to different people at different times, it can add a kind of stage fright to your problems as you try to stay consistent with the excuses you've used in the past. This often adds more anxiety because you have to stay alert enough to not contradict your story and also to not use the same excuse with the same person too often. It's often harder, and more anxiety provoking, to try to maintain a fake explanation than it is to simply express the truth as you best know it. The truth will set you free.

Increased Social Isolation

If your anxiety makes it difficult for you to meet friends at a restaurant or go to a party at their home and you want to keep it a secret, then you have to come up with some excuse to explain why you won't attend. If you did this just once, maybe no one would be the wiser. But people who struggle to keep their anxiety troubles a secret from their friends often get into a pattern of making excuses for their refusal to accept social invitations, and friends will notice the pattern. Anxious people trying to hide their anxiety will make so many excuses that they often fall back on implausible reasons, like their grandmother died for the third time this year. Friends will often conclude, after a series of refusals without a plausible explanation for the turndowns, that you just don't want to spend time with them, and then your friendships may wither.

Paradoxical Influences on Symptoms

What you resist, persists. The more people focus on hiding their anxiety symptoms, the more trouble they are likely to have with them. People tend to experience precisely the symptoms they hope not to have, and their efforts at hiding their troubles are likely to increase the frequency and severity of their symptoms.

People with social anxiety disorder have many more observable symptoms—sweating, blushing, trembling, voice cracking—than do people with panic disorder or generalized anxiety disorder. Why do you suppose people with social anxiety disorder have so many more observable symptoms? These are the symptoms that they most dislike and hope to avoid! It's a characteristic of the anxiety disorders that *you get what you don't want.* Try to keep them a secret, and they're likely to blossom even more.

Self-Disclosure: Why Would I Do That?

Self-disclosure involves revealing some aspects of your anxiety trouble to selected people rather than keeping them a secret from everyone. Most people don't like the idea of self-disclosure, and maybe you don't either. "It's none of their business!" my clients have often told me. "They don't have the right [or need] to know!"

That's perfectly true. Self-disclosure isn't something you do because others have a right or need to know your business. It's none of their business at all. The only good reason to do self-disclosure would be to help *your* business of living. Self-disclosure is done only for your benefit, not for others.

It's a difficult decision to make, to voluntarily disclose some of your anxiety troubles to a trusted friend or loved one. I always ask clients, "Who knows about this problem?" and it's frequently shocking to discover how total the secrecy is. Even people in long-term relationships and marriages often keep a lot of anxiety secret from their partners, who may only know a few generalities.

Once in a while, a client will respond to this question by telling me that they have shared their anxiety trouble with someone. I've learned to shut my mouth and wait when they tell me that. Almost always, my client will then say something like this: "And you know, it's funny—I never panic in front of that person!"

A woman called me about a problem in which her hands shook when she got nervous in front of others. She was terribly ashamed of her hands shaking and had kept this a secret her entire adult life by avoiding any activity—eating, writing, telephone usage—that required the use of her hands when others were nearby. As a result, she had many phobias that restricted her life.

We had a natural opportunity for exposure practice the very first session, when it came time to write me a check. Usually she would have found some excuse to write it out of view, but she agreed to write it in front of me. Her hands didn't shake when she wrote it. She said that her hands didn't shake because she had twenty-five blank checks with her, and she felt sure she could produce at least one good check out of twenty-five.

I asked if she was willing to try an experiment, and she agreed. I asked her to rip up the check she had just written and rip up twenty-three of the remaining twenty-four blank checks as well. She was surprised but agreed, and together we ripped up the checks. Now she had one check left, just one try at writing a legible check. She wrote the remaining check without any shaking.

I asked her to explain the failure of her hands to shake when she had only one check to use. She said that her hands didn't shake this time because I already knew about her hand-shaking problem, and she had nothing to hide from me.

Here we can see the trick fully revealed.

- She was ashamed of her anxiety symptom of hands shaking.

- She went to great lengths to hide it.

- The more she hid it, the more anxious she became.

- The more anxious she became, the more her hands shook.

- When in front of someone who knew about her hands shaking, her hands didn't shake.

There's a lot of power in doing self-disclosure, power that can help you rein in the troubles you have with anxiety and worry if you decide to go this way.

You don't need to assume that self-disclosure will help you or blindly follow this suggestion. Keep an open mind and do a cost-benefit analysis of the possible benefits of self-disclosure. Here's how:

1. Identify one person in your life who clearly has your best interests at heart, someone who has your back as much as, or more than, anyone else you know. This should be someone with whom you've used excuses and deception to hide your anxiety.

2. Consider the benefits you get from keeping your anxiety troubles a secret from this person. This usually has to do with sparing you the embarrassment you expect to experience from revealing your troubles and how you expect that person to react. Answer the following questions in your notebook:

- How has this person reacted in the past when you have done or revealed something that you found embarrassing, shameful, or negative? What was the worst thing they did in response? How did that affect you and for how long?

- What is the worst thing you suppose this person might do if you disclosed some of the trouble you have with anxiety and explained how it has affected your relationship (for instance, how it's led you to avoid certain activities with them)?

- Are there any good ways this person might react to your self-disclosure?

3. Review the description of the five negative side effects above. Do you see signs that you have experienced some of these negative effects? If so, how might your life, and your friendship,

improve if you could remove them by doing some self-disclosure?

4. Throughout your entire life, what was your most embarrassing experience? How did you handle it? What was the ultimate result of feeling so embarrassed?

Take plenty of time to answer the questions above so you can form an opinion about all the possible costs and benefits of disclosing some of your anxiety and worry troubles to this one, trusted friend. I think there's a good chance that many people will come to realize that they've kept their anxiety a secret out of fear and a bias toward imagining the negative while overlooking the positive. Taking the time to do this cost-benefit analysis might help you overcome that.

If, after doing the analysis and giving it some thought, you are willing to consider experimenting with some self-disclosure to this person, here are some suggestions for how to proceed.

1. Tell your friend that you have something you want to discuss, and set a time to get together in the very near future for this specific purpose. Your friend might be curious, so let them know that you don't want to borrow money or complain about their behavior, just that you have something on your mind to talk over.

2. Recognize that you will probably feel nervous as the time approaches. Don't try to talk yourself out of feeling nervous or argue with yourself about it. Review some of the tips for handling anticipatory worry in chapter 6 if you feel the need.

3. When the time comes, get right to the point. If your friend knows anything about your anxiety, mention that it's about that. If they know nothing about your anxiety, explain that you don't know if they recognize it, but that sometimes you have trouble with anxiety and that this is the topic you want to discuss.

4. If you want your friend to keep this conversation private and not share it with others, ask for that.

5. Give your friend a sample description of how you sometimes experience anxiety in ways that lead you to limit your activities. Tell them that you're dealing with this as best as you can and you didn't want to give the impression that you didn't want to spend time together, because you value the friendship. And, if you're willing, offer to be more candid in the future when you don't want to do something due to anxiety, rather than make an excuse.

Outsmart Your Anxious Brain

6. Your friend may ask, "How can I help?" Explain that the biggest help would be knowing that you can be candid when the anxiety troubles you and knowing that your friend will understand that your turning down an invitation isn't a reflection on your friendship, but it's just you having trouble with anxiety.

It's a difficult decision for people to make—to break the secrecy that you might have maintained for years and voluntarily disclose it to a trusted friend. Don't rush! Do the cost-benefit analysis I describe above, and see if you might find some benefit in doing self-disclosure. Clients I've worked with usually have a great deal of fear and resistance to doing self-disclosure, and yet I've never seen it fail to produce a good result when they did.

Thinking It Over

When people feel ashamed of their troubles with anxiety and worry, they tend to try to hide the problem. And the more they try to hide the problem, the more shame they experience. Reviewing all the costs and benefits associated with keeping your anxiety a secret from people who care for you might reveal some advantages to breaking the secrecy and doing some self-disclosure with those people.

In the next chapter, we'll look at the problem of how people get tricked into a struggle for control when they experience worry and anxiety and how they can play their hand differently to obtain a better outcome.

Chapter 11

Control Actions and Accept Feelings

When you struggle with a chronic anxiety disorder, you probably focus a lot on how you feel. That's understandable because you want so much to feel better.

Anxiety can trick you into judging your day, or week, by how you felt. If you felt good, you judge that as a good day, and if you felt anxious, you judge that as a bad day. Even worse, anxiety can trick you into trying to control your feelings, and that hardly ever ends well.

● We don't control our feelings. The only thing we can really control is what we do. And you'll probably be better off by controlling, and focusing on, what you do, rather than how you feel.

If you've ever visited an eye doctor to have your vision checked, you've probably had this experience. The eye doctor has you look through a set of lenses at an eye chart, asking, as she switches through different settings, "Better here...or better here?"

I'm going to ask you a similar question. I'd like you to recall a time when you were in a situation that scared you. Maybe you were on board an airplane, giving a talk at your church or workplace, at a party with a group of strangers, or trying to relax in a crowded restaurant or theater.

First, I'd like you to recall such a time when you were in that anxiety-provoking situation and your attention was focused on how you felt. Your focus was on all your "internals": what you were feeling emotionally; what your heart was doing; how your breathing felt; the sensations in your stomach; and the pictures, images, and thoughts that crossed your mind while you were in the situation.

Then I'd like you to recall a different time when you faced the same kind of situational anxiety and were much more focused on some activity or interaction with the physical environment around you. This would be a time when you were focused on or engaged with something outside of yourself, dealing with the objects, people, and activities that existed around and outside of you.

Where did you feel better? Which one do you prefer? Better here (when you were actively engaged with the people and objects in your immediate environment)…or better here (when your attention was focused on how you felt inside)?

Most people seem to feel better when they're involved in the present moment, in their interaction with the people and objects around them, using their hands and feet and voice, when they're more focused on involvement with their immediate environment than they are with how they feel (and think) inside themselves. It doesn't always hold true. It's not guaranteed or written in stone. But it's more likely than not to be the case in most situations.

✶   We're much more likely to feel anxious and uncomfortable when we're focused on changing and resisting our internal sensations, emotions, and thoughts. We're much less likely to feel anxious and uncomfortable when we're focused on our activity and involvement with the world around us.

When you're anxiously focused on yourself, it's not usually problem solving or planning that you're engaged in. It's usually a constant scanning, looking for trouble inside yourself, a repetitive review of what-if thoughts and concerns about the future and a struggle to stop feeling so anxious. When you're so focused on the thoughts in your head, it's like you're continually drawn up to the attic, rearranging furniture and boxes of old stuff that you probably won't use and don't need. Dinner is ready, and it's on the table waiting for you. It's good food, food you'll enjoy, once you get downstairs to the dining table. There's conversation too that might well be enjoyable. But rearranging the furniture is such a habit that it can keep you in the attic without noticing what you're missing.

Focus on What You Do

The most important influence on how we feel, emotionally and physically, is how we act.

- If I run away from something, I probably feel more afraid over time. If I deal with something I've been avoiding, I probably feel better.

Feelings follow behavior.

But we're so prone to getting tricked into focusing on our immediate thoughts and feelings, hoping that somehow we can directly control what we feel and think, that we end up feeling worse rather than better for all our efforts.

New clients often tell me that they need confidence, and that's why they've come to see me. They have the idea that "*First*, I have to feel confident, and *then* I can do those things I fear." They think they need to first become confident about flying, driving, public speaking, or whatever they fear so that then they can approach the feared activity. It's like they've come in to buy a can of confidence. But of course, I don't have any cans of confidence to sell them. This idea, that we first have to feel confident *before* we can tackle a feared activity, is a major factor in maintaining situational anxiety and the phobias that come with it.

People gain confidence by taking action, by doing things that they're not so familiar or skillful with. Recall how you became confident riding a bicycle. You probably did that by first riding it fearfully, and poorly, with little or no skill because you were doing something unfamiliar. Over time, you started riding less poorly and awkwardly, and eventually you became so skilled at riding your bicycle, so familiar with the process, that it started to feel good to you. You paid more attention to holding the handlebars, adjusting your speed, and the scenery in front of you and less and less to how you felt. That's how children acquire confidence in their ability to ride bicycles.

First you rode the bicycle, poorly and nervously. Then later, you felt confident as a result of the effort and time you invested in riding it poorly. Feelings follow behavior. If you wait until you feel confident before riding the bicycle, you might never learn to use it. What stops fearful flyers from getting on airplanes is the idea that they have to first lose their fear *before* they can fly. It's actually okay to fly while afraid. That's how fearful flyers gain confidence and lose their fear: by working with the fear rather than against it.

● You can get both these things—confidence and a life in which you're able to do what you want, where you want—but not in that order. You generally need to do this in the opposite order. First, you do the things you fear, and then you come to feel confident. Confidence isn't a commodity you acquire. It's something that naturally develops out of the actions you take.

This fundamental misunderstanding—that people need to become confident before they engage in the activities they fear—tricks people into behaving in ways that maintain their fears and phobias. The socially anxious person who fears small talk at parties; the person who fears insects, birds, or snakes; the person who fears highway driving—they get stuck because they hope to lose their fears before they go encounter what they fear. That desire to lose your fears before you engage in the feared activity is what keeps you phobic!

Feelings follow behavior. Focus on what you do, rather than what you feel or think. You can probably already see that the Rule of Opposites will tell you this: first, go do those things that you fear, and later, you will become less afraid and more confident. Allow yourself to experience fear, and that's how you will develop confidence.

Issues of Control

People who struggle with fears and phobias often have a lot of trouble with issues of control.

I don't mean this the way you have probably heard it before. Friends, family, and anyone with whom you've discussed your difficulties with anxiety might have told you that you have "control issues" because you insist on certain details in your activities together—whose car you'll travel in together, who will do the driving, what types of roads you will take, whether to arrive at the party early or late, where to eat, where to sit in a theater or restaurant, and so on.

Outsmart Your Anxious Brain

It's true that anxious people are often concerned with these issues and want to do things "their way." It's not, however, because they're bossy people who just want to control others. It's very different from that.

People with fears and phobias often try to control things that are outside of their usual range of control. They try to control events and situations outside of themselves, hoping that this will bring them the internal feelings of comfort they want. Here's an example of what I mean.

People who fear flying usually try to control a number of things in their environment that are outside their span of control. Here are some examples of what fearful flyers do in an attempt to lower their fear level:

- Watching the Weather Channel in the days and weeks before a flight

- Watching for terrorists at the gate and on the plane

- Watching the engines, the wings, and various other parts of the plane in flight

- Trying to be healthier than usual before a flight—better sleep and rest, and more emphasis on nutrition and exercise

- Trying to be a "better person" before the flight—more pleasant and cooperative, more law-abiding, more considerate of others—in hopes that the universe, and the deity, will recognize their improved behavior and reward them with an easier, safer flight

- Picking the details of the flight—which airline, what time of day, what day of the week, and so forth—in an attempt to improve the odds of a safe or comfortable trip

- Waiting until the last moment to board in an attempt to minimize the duration of their fear

- Scrutinizing the pilot when possible in an attempt to feel satisfied that the pilot appears to be happy, healthy, well adjusted, rested, well trained, and so on. I've known clients who asked to see pictures of the pilot's children, thinking that this would be evidence of a motivated pilot!

- Engaging in superstitious behaviors, like wearing lucky shirts

If you have a specific fear or phobia—like flying, parties, public speaking, driving, animals, or whatever—what habitual actions do you usually take to prepare yourself for an encounter with what you fear? Make a list in your notebook.

These efforts, unfortunately, don't usually bring people the increased comfort they want. People often feel worse and experience more anxiety as a result of their efforts to control because they fail to stay within the parameters of their role. Here's what I mean by that.

We all cycle through a variety of roles, probably every day. In a single day, I might find myself in the roles of:

father or spouse (when I'm with family)

doctor (when I'm working with a client)

patient (when I'm visiting my physician)

customer (when I'm shopping)

passenger (when I take the train home)

driver (when I drive to a store)

teacher (when I give a lecture)

student (when I attend a lecture)

Each of these different roles comes with its own set of rules, responsibilities, and controls. When I'm driving my car, it's my job to do everything I can to ensure a safe ride. I do that by behaving in particular ways: I monitor traffic all around me; I maintain a safe speed; I use my lights, mirrors, and signals in ways designed to promote safety; I choose an appropriate route. I can control all these things. The role of driver comes with a lot of controls.

I play a very different role when I'm a passenger on a train. I probably don't have a designated seat and can sit anywhere I choose. No one counts on me to make the train safer because that's not the job of a passenger. I don't need to monitor the speed of the train or any of the decisions the operator makes, not only because that's not my job, but also because I don't have any special training or skills that would make me a good judge of the conductor's choices.

If I do take on the responsibility of a driver when I'm only a passenger, it's likely to lead me to feel more anxious rather than less because I become focused on second-guessing and trying to change the behavior of the person who is actually doing the driving. I become the stereotypical backseat driver. This makes me (and probably my driver as well) less comfortable rather than more because I'm trying to control the car when I don't have access to the controls. I'm resisting, rather than embracing, my role as a passenger.

People have phobias because *they fail to embrace the particular role* in which they're cast.

If you want to fly on a commercial airline, your role is passenger. The airline will tell you when to get on the plane, where to sit, when you can use the bathroom and when you can't, when you can have a beverage and when you can't, which bathroom you can form a line for and which one you can't, and when to get off the plane. What's the role of a passenger on a commercial airline? There's nothing you need to do but sit there until they tell you that you've arrived at your destination and it's time to disembark. You're baggage that breathes!

Fearful flyers resist this and try to feel "in control" of something. This tends to make them feel more anxious and less comfortable, however, because they don't really have the training or the responsibility to identify terrorists, notice something wrong with an engine, or detect hazardous weather. Their efforts to control things that they can't control usually make them feel more anxious rather than less.

The fearful flyer tries to have controls that don't come with the role of passenger and feels worse for those efforts. We see the problem play out in the opposite manner with a fear of public speaking.

The role of public speaker carries a variety of powers. The audience and the sponsors delegate to the speaker the power to:

- start the meeting

- shape the outline and order of the material presented

- call for breaks and for questions

- use gestures, various volume levels, pauses, variations in the rate of speaking, and emotionality to maintain the interest of the audience

- look at the audience to judge their level of interest and comprehension

- ask questions of the audience and invite a dialogue if the speaker desires

- run the meeting in almost every way.

The audience has agreed to listen and allow the speaker to speak. But the typical fearful speaker doesn't want any of that authority! The fearful speaker would rather phone it in, send a memo, or even read it aloud without looking at or interacting with the audience. Here we see the reverse of the problem encountered by the fearful flyer. The fearful speaker has been delegated a variety of powers and, in thinking that using them would make him more nervous, avoids using any of them.

So a fearful speaker often avoids making eye contact with members of the audience. He then feels more anxious rather than less because he gets caught up in his own head rather than interacting with the audience. A fearful speaker often hurries through the presentation, barely giving himself enough time to pause and breathe, because he thinks the audience will demand that he speak rapidly and continuously. This also makes him more nervous and frequently gives rise to literally running out of air. Since we talk by making air vibrate through our vocal cords, that's going to be a problem! A fearful speaker will read from notes, rather than look up at the audience and talk. He'll try to remain calm and unemotional in an effort to suppress his anxiety. He approaches the act of public speaking as if it's a test of his ability to avoid looking anxious, rather than an occasion to give the audience the information they've come for.

When you confront a feared situation, activity, or object, it's often your resistance to your assigned role and the degree of control it gives you that causes your trouble. The more you accept your designated role—passenger, speaker, or whatever it is—and act in concert with the degree of control it provides, the more calm you will come to feel.

This is how you can help yourself with feared situations. Look at the controls that do or don't come with the role you play in that situation. Control what you can without trying to control things that you can't. In this way, a fearful flyer will become more comfortable by giving up those activities by which he tries to make the flight safer because they're not within his ability or job description. A fearful speaker will become more comfortable by directing the audience's attention and giving them the information they came for, rather than trying to control or hide the anxiety he feels.

Situational anxiety can be reduced by more fully embracing the control that comes with your role, and nothing more or less. Here's how you can help yourself do this.

Evaluate the situation in which you customarily feel anxious by determining what you do and don't control in that situation. Take out your notebook and make a list for your feared situation, be it an airplane ride, a presentation, or making small talk at a party, of what you do and don't control in that situation.

Consider questions like these as you make your list. Do I control:

- what thoughts I have?

- my physical sensations?

- what emotions I feel?

- what I say?

- what others say?

- what I do with my arms, legs, hands, feet, and voice?

- what others do?

Control what you can control and allow yourself to accept whatever you don't control. That's all any of us can do in life.

So if you're giving a presentation to a group, you can control the way you present the material and the way you act. You can't control their reactions. When you give a presentation, you're giving that group a gift. Some of them might like it a lot, and others not so much. That isn't up to you.

And when you're experiencing the situations, cues, and triggers that so often precipitate an anxious or worried reaction, remind yourself again of the question from the eye doctor: Where is a good place for my attention and energy right now? Is it better here (focused on my interaction with the world around me) or better here (focused on all my bodily symptoms and sensations)?

Thinking It Over

Because we're so aware of our thoughts and feelings, we naturally tend to evaluate our lives by how we think and feel and try to control it. This generally makes us less comfortable. We tend to want to have confidence about new or challenging activities and situations first, before we act, when in reality confidence generally comes *after* sustained action. Confidence, and comfort, will come, but they're generally last and people get so tricked by trying to have them first. The only thing we really control is what we do, and this is the best place for our focus and efforts.

In the next chapter, we'll look at how people often get tricked when they seek to do exposure practice.

Chapter 12

Feel the Fear and Let It Pass

In this chapter, we will consider the most counterintuitive aspect of recovery from a chronic anxiety disorder, the aspect that most frequently confuses and misleads sufferers. There are, unfortunately, even lots of professional therapists who fail to understand this key point. It's also widely misunderstood by physicians and other health professionals who aren't specialists in mental health but often play an important role in the treatment. It's of critical importance to the success of exposure practice.

Don't try to get rid of your fears, or even calm down, while you're doing exposure practice. When you get tricked into opposing, fleeing, and otherwise trying to get rid of your fears during exposure practice, it undermines the benefits you will get from exposure and makes the problem worse.

Instead, let yourself feel afraid. Allow yourself to experience the scary thoughts, emotions, and physical sensations without trying to get rid of them or distract yourself from them. Practice, a step at a time, with situations that elicit your panic, worry, and anxiety and allow yourself to feel afraid. Do not attempt to oppose or interrupt the anxiety that ensues. Follow these steps:

1. Spend time with what you fear: the object, activity, situation, or even thoughts.

2. Reduce your use of safety behaviors, people, and objects as much as you are willing. Work toward having none of them during exposure practice.

3. Get afraid.

4. Allow yourself to experience the fear without trying to get rid of it.

5. Stay with it until the fear level comes down some, mostly on its own. Let the fear leave, at least in part, before you do.

6. Review your results. What happened as a result of exposure, and what didn't happen? How does that compare with what you anticipated?

7. Repeat as necessary, on a regular basis.

People often misunderstand what exposure therapy is all about. They understand that they're supposed to go spend time with what scares them, rather than avoid it. But they sometimes think that when they do exposure practice, they're supposed to go to the feared situation—maybe highway driving, shopping in a crowded mall, or riding an elevator—and try not to be afraid somehow, maybe by distracting themselves, trying to reason with their fears, or doing some other safety behavior. Even when they understand that they're not supposed to resist the fear, it's such a natural instinct that they find themselves resisting anyway.

Harry had a strong fear of highway driving. He spent a couple of hours each day driving to and from work by local roads when it would have been so much faster to drive on the highway. He was working hard to overcome this fear with exposure practice. One day he reported to me that he had done his previous week's homework of three sessions, thirty minutes each, of highway driving. I asked him how it went. "Great!" he said, "I didn't have a single panic attack!"

"Don't be disappointed," I said. "Keep trying!" We had a good laugh over that, but I had a serious point. He needed to go have some panic attacks while driving on the highway in order to retrain his amygdala. He needed to discover that, however unpleasant the experience was, he could handle it, keep driving, and allow the panic feelings to subside rather than try to make them go away. He needed, in particular, to allow his amygdala to discover that. That's how exposure practice works. It's not about trying to become unafraid; it's about letting yourself feel afraid and allowing it to gradually subside. It's about losing your fear of fear.

Is It Safe to Do This?

You can review your own situation to determine whether exposure is safe. First, recognize that you're dealing with a fear that you want to overcome. This by itself puts the fear into a special category. The people who come to my office for help in overcoming a fear have already decided that it would be beneficial to them to do so. They see that the fear isn't making any kind of useful contribution to their lives. It's preventing them from living their lives the way they want, and it's not making them any safer. Nobody has ever come to see me for help overcoming their fear of running across an eight-lane highway or jumping into the lion cage at the zoo, because that would be dangerous! People don't typically want to get rid of a fear that actually protects them. They want to get rid of a fear that tricks them.

Second, carefully review and answer all the questions in chapter 4. They will guide you through a review of your actual experience with your fear. They will help you consider what the fear has actually done to you in the past, rather than what you feared it might do or thought that it almost did. If you can see that the fear has historically been scaring you without ever delivering on its threats of harm, that also indicates that your problem is a good candidate for exposure practice.

If, after reviewing both these steps, you're not clear whether your problem is suitable for exposure, then I suggest you arrange a consultation with a psychotherapist experienced in treating these problems. The websites of both the Anxiety and Depression Association of America and the Association for Behavioral and Cognitive Therapies have useful directories of therapists listed by geographical area.

How Can You Let Yourself Get Afraid?

It's not easy, or pleasant, but most people can do it. Because our natural instinct is to resist or avoid fear, it helps to get your purpose, of hanging out with the fear, clearly fixed in your mind. Whenever I go with a group of fearful flyers on an exposure flight, someone usually asks if it would be okay to bring their Xanax, or their comfort animal, or videos to distract them during the flight. I like to summarize our intention for the group this way.

> Let's remember why we're flying to Detroit [or wherever we're going]. We don't have any business in Detroit. No one will meet us at the airport. We won't even leave the airfield to go anywhere. No sooner will we get there than we'll turn around and take another flight home. What is the reason we're going? Only to get afraid!

This helps them recognize that it wouldn't make much sense to spend all the time, effort, and money they invested in the fear-of-flying workshop and then do something to reduce their fear. The whole point of the flight is to get afraid and work with the fear, rather than against it. That's the point of all exposure practice.

People often want to keep some of their safety behaviors during the exposure practice and gradually phase them out, rather than drop them all at once. If this is what it takes to allow you to get started with exposure practice, then do so. Be aware, however, that in order to progress, you need to be systematically reducing your reliance on safety behaviors and not keeping them long term. Also keep in mind that people usually need to become afraid during exposure in order for it to be useful. If your reliance on safety behaviors prevents you from feeling afraid during exposure practice, then it's time to get rid of a few more of them.

Ways to allow yourself to feel afraid and work *with* it, rather than against it, include:

- AWARE steps (chapter 4)

- Journals (chapter 7)

- Symptom Inventory (chapter 7)

- Humoring the what-if thoughts (chapters 5 and 6)

- Belly breathing (chapter 3)

Planning Your Exposure Practice

Work with one fear at a time. If you have multiple fears and phobias, focus first on one of them, perhaps the one that offers the most opportunities for regular practice and that can be broken down into a set of small tasks. Driving usually offers lots of opportunities for working one step at a time, and flying not so many.

Prepare yourself with a fire drill. Literally pretend you are in your feared situation, becoming powerfully afraid, and run through the responses you will use. This will help you respond more automatically with accepting, rather than resisting, responses.

Don't combine exposure with daily tasks. If you're going to drive on the highway, it might occur to you to combine the exposure with a drive you have to make anyway, but I suggest you do the exposure all by itself. Similarly, if you're going to take a first flight after years of avoidance, it's better to take a short flight just for that purpose, rather than piggybacking it onto a business trip or vacation. You want to be free to let yourself get afraid and not be burdened by completing some other task at the same time.

Break it into small steps. List all the variables that might influence how difficult an exposure task might be. For instance, the variables affecting a driving fear probably include:

- distance
- type of road
- time of day and how much traffic
- weather
- driving with a passenger or alone

Build success into your program by starting with tasks that appear less anxiety provoking and then moving on to more challenging situations.

Schedule in advance. Plan your exposure schedule a week in advance. Commit yourself ahead of time to the specific days and times you will do exposure, rather than making that decision each day after you wake up. An hour is usually a sufficient amount of time for most exposure practice. However, be sure to schedule it at times when you can extend your practice, in case you're quite anxious right at the end of the hour. In that case, it would be advantageous to stay longer, so the anxiety can leave before you do.

Decide in advance what you'll do. If you're driving, decide in advance the destination you'll drive to. If you don't plan this, you might drive until you feel anxious and then turn around. If you do that, you're getting relief by leaving, and that's unhelpful. If you're riding elevators, plan to spend a certain amount of time in the elevator before you get off. You don't have to be moving all that time or even have the door closed. But stay on the elevator for a particular period of time. Otherwise, you'll get your relief by leaving the elevator, and that's the opposite of helpful!

Make sure your exposure is "relevant." If you have anxiety meeting new people and go to a party but hang out in the corner and don't introduce yourself to anyone, you're actually avoiding what you fear, and that's unhelpful. It's the same thing if you're afraid of standing in long grocery lines and go to the supermarket, but only when it's unlikely to be busy. Get practice with precisely what you fear.

Doing exposure if you have no specific cues or phobias. Sometimes people see no obvious pattern to their panic attacks. They just seem to come at varied times without any obvious external cue. Use the Panic Journal (available online at http://www.newharbinger.com/41993) to see if you can notice any other patterns. It might be that your cues are internal, rather than external. These can be harder to notice. Maybe you tend to panic when you're bored, doing something that's not very interesting to you, or have a full stomach. Maybe you panic in response to certain thoughts or sensations regardless of where you are or what you're doing. There's usually some kind of pattern, even if it's only the appearance of a thought like, *What if I panic now?* You could then do exposure to those internal cues.

Doing exposure with fearful thoughts. Sometimes people ask questions like this: "I panic when I think about death. What can I do? I can't expose myself to death!" No, but you can do an exposure to having the *thought* about death, or whatever thought is your cue. It's the thought that triggers the panic, not death or another calamity. Chapter 6 suggests a variety of ways to do humorous exposure to thoughts.

It's common for people to feel afraid simply in response to our conversation about doing exposure practice. That often happens when I'm discussing a drive with a client who fears driving or a flight with a client who fears flying. It happens when I send an e-mail notice to a fearful flyers group and they see that the subject line pertains to flying! They become afraid just from the ideas expressed in our conversation. When this happens, it's another opportunity to use thoughts for exposure practice. You can repeat aloud the thoughts that scare you, maybe fifteen or twenty repetitions, until they start to lose their power to disturb.

This is not a test; it's practice. Frequently a client will mention, when we're discussing steps they can take in exposure, "That'll be a good test!"

Outsmart Your Anxious Brain

Exposure is never a test. Test means these things: "Pencils down! Turn in your papers! This result will be in your record forever! Do you pass or fail?" Exposure is always practice. There are always more opportunities to practice, a step at a time, for your own ongoing benefit.

An anxiety disorder is not a disease. An anxiety disorder is an overblown version of ordinary anxiety. Ordinary anxiety is present in all of us, for all our lives. It's necessary to our survival. Don't set your sights on eliminating all anxiety. It's neither desirable nor possible. Instead, focus on getting better at accepting, and working with, anxiety in all its forms. We don't "*cure*" anxiety the way we cure an infectious disease, by eliminating it. We make a good "*recovery*" from an anxiety disorder by losing our fear of fear.

Thinking It Over

The most counterintuitive aspect of exposure practice is that it calls upon you to willingly let yourself become afraid and refrain from responses that will interrupt or stop the anxiety. Exposure isn't about "toughing it out" when you become afraid. It's about allowing yourself to feel afraid, staying in place, and giving the fear some time to pass. This is how you can retrain your amygdala and lose your fear of fear.

Congratulations! You've read the book and hopefully tried some of the exercises and experiments. Now it's time, if you're ready, to begin putting these ten simple ways into practice on a regular basis. Come join the ranks of those who are no longer so afraid of feeling afraid!

Postscript

So those are the ten simple ways you can use to beat the worry trick. You can use them to change how you usually respond to the signs and symptoms of chronic worry and anxiety and, in so doing, change your future experience for the better.

This is an action-oriented book, and so I tried to make the ten ways as clear and specific as possible. That doesn't mean that they're easy to do. They're often hard, but if you take it a step at a time and persist, I think you will find it gradually gets easier.

It's so tempting to "just get through" the experience of intense anxiety and panic that people often fail to notice how, one moment at a time, they're giving up the opportunity to live their life the way they want. They get tricked into making so many bad trades, giving up their long-term freedom in exchange for a few moments of temporary comfort, that they almost forget what it's like to feel free to live and do as they wish.

Sometimes, when people watch a scary movie, they get more afraid than they bargained for and want to reduce the fear. They could flee the theater, but they're often with friends, and it would be inconvenient to leave. Instead, they do various things to "just get through" the movie. They distract themselves with games and texts on their phone, they remind themselves that "it's only a movie," and sometimes they even grab on to the person sitting next to them. If they came in with that person, that's probably okay to do.

"Getting through" a scary movie is a reasonable strategy because no movie is so important that you simply must see it. Even when a person decides they won't ever go to see another scary movie, they give up next to nothing in life because it's entertainment and entirely optional.

It's so tempting, when you're in a struggle with a chronic anxiety disorder, to use the same strategy and "just get through it." That's when you make all those bad trades in which you get a little temporary comfort while giving up your long-term freedom. But this is very different from getting through a movie. When you get tricked into making these bad trades, you're applying the strategy "just get through it" not to a movie, but to your life.

That's the worst and cruelest trick of all. Don't fall for it! This might be the only life you get. So here are the ten simple ways you can beat the worry trick. You can use them to do something different—so different that it's the opposite—and regain your freedom to live life the way you want.

I frequently get e-mails from people all around the world who tell me of their efforts and their successes at regaining their freedom after a long struggle with a chronic anxiety disorder. I hope someday to get one from you!

Endnotes

Introduction

1 David Carbonell, *Panic Attack Workbook: A Guided Program for Beating the Panic Trick* (Berkeley, CA: Ulysses Press: 2004)

2 David Carbonell, *The Worry Trick: How Your Brain Tricks You into Expecting the Worst and What You Can Do About It* (Oakland, CA: New Harbinger Publications, 2016)

3 Claire Weekes, *Hope and Health for Your Nerves* (New York: Penguin Books, 1969)

Chapter 4

4 Catherine Pittman and Elizabeth Karle, *Extinguishing Anxiety: Whole Brain Strategies to Relieve Fear and Stress* (South Bend, IN: Foliadeux Press, 2009).

5 Aaron Beck, Gary Emery, and Ruth Greenberg, *Anxiety Disorders and Phobias: A Cognitive Perspective* (New York: Basic Books, 1985).

Chapter 7

6   Daniel Wegner, *White Bears and Other Unwanted Thoughts: Supression, Obsession, and the Psychology of Mental Control* (New York: Viking Penguin, 1989).

7   Lee Baer, *The Imp of the Mind: Exploring the Silent Epidemic of Obsessive Bad Thoughts* (New York: The Penguin Group, 2001).

David A. Carbonell, PhD, is a clinical psychologist who specializes in treating anxiety in all its forms. He is author of *Panic Attacks Workbook*, *The Worry Trick*, and *Fear of Flying Workbook*. He is "coach" of the popular self-help site www.anxietycoach. com, and has taught workshops on the treatment of anxiety disorders to more than 9,000 professional psychotherapists in the U.S. and abroad. He is a long-standing member of the Anxiety and Depression Association of America, and a frequent presenter at their annual conferences. He received his doctorate in clinical psychology from DePaul University in 1985, and has maintained a practice devoted to the treatment of anxiety disorders since 1990. He lives in Chicago, IL, with his wife and a pair of rescue dogs. In his spare time, he is founding member of The Therapy Players, an improvisational comedy troupe of professional psychotherapists which performs at clubs, theaters, and mental health conferences throughout the Chicago area.

Foreword writer **Martin N. Seif, PhD,** is cofounder of the Anxiety and Depression Association of America, and was a member of its board of directors from 1977 through 1991. He maintains a private practice in New York, NY; and Greenwich, CT; and is coauthor of *What Every Therapist Needs to Know About Anxiety Disorders* and *Overcoming Unwanted Intrusive Thoughts*.

Real change *is* possible

For more than forty-five years, New Harbinger has published proven-effective self-help books and pioneering workbooks to help readers of all ages and backgrounds improve mental health and well-being, and achieve lasting personal growth. In addition, our spirituality books offer profound guidance for deepening awareness and cultivating healing, self-discovery, and fulfillment.

Founded by psychologist Matthew McKay and Patrick Fanning, New Harbinger is proud to be an independent, employee-owned company. Our books reflect our core values of integrity, innovation, commitment, sustainability, compassion, and trust. Written by leaders in the field and recommended by therapists worldwide, New Harbinger books are practical, accessible, and provide real tools for real change.

 new**harbinger**publications

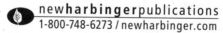

Register your **new harbinger** titles for additional benefits!

When you register your **new harbinger** title—purchased in any format, from any source—you get access to benefits like the following:

- Downloadable accessories like printable worksheets and extra content
- Instructional videos and audio files
- Information about updates, corrections, and new editions

Not every title has accessories, but we're adding new material all the time.

Access free accessories in 3 easy steps:

1. Sign in at NewHarbinger.com (or **register** to create an account).

2. Click on **register a book**. Search for your title and click the **register** button when it appears.

3. Click on the **book cover or title** to go to its details page. Click on **accessories** to view and access files.

That's all there is to it!

If you need help, visit:

NewHarbinger.com/accessories

new harbinger
CELEBRATING
40 YEARS